THE MEDIA DESIGN BOOK
IDEAS AND PROJECTS FOR AUDIO, VIDEO, AND COMPUTER COMPONENTS FOR THE HOME AND OFFICE

Philip Mazzurco

COLLIER BOOKS
Macmillan Publishing Company
New York

A QUARTO BOOK

Copyright © 1984 by Quarto Marketing Ltd.

All rights reserved under the Pan-American and International Copyright Conventions. No part of this book may be reproduced or transmitted in any form or by any means electronic or mechanical, including photocopying, recording or by any information storage and retrieval system, without permission in writing from the Publisher.

Macmillan Publishing Company
866 Third Avenue
New York, New York 10022

Library of Congress Cataloging in Publication Data
Mazzurco, Philip.
The media design book.
(A Quarto book)
1. Home video systems—Amateurs' manuals.
2. Microcomputers—Amateurs' manuals. 3. Stereophonic sound systems—Amateurs' manuals. I. Title.
[TK9961.M39 1984b]   621.38   84-7105

ISBN 0-02-008640-7 (pbk.)

THE MEDIA DESIGN BOOK
was produced and prepared by Quarto Marketing Ltd.
New York, NY 10010

Editor: Naomi Black
Art Director/Designer: Richard Boddy
Editorial Assistant: Mary Forsell
Technical Advice and Consultation: Cliff Shumaker, Hal Pontez

Front cover photograph by Derrick and Love

Typeset by BPE Graphics, Inc.
Color separations by Hong Kong Scanner Craft Company Ltd.
Printed and bound in Hong Kong by Leefung-Asco Printers Ltd.

The Media Design Book is also published in a hardcover edition by Macmillan Publishing Company.

For Mom and Dad

ACKNOWLEDGMENTS

For ■ CLIFF SHUMAKER and HAL PONTEZ, The Audio Consultant, a special thanks for their significant contribution of technical advice and consultation generously given throughout this entire project ■ JOHN HAWKINS, whose unfailing encouragement, professional advice, and friendship saw me through some of the more desperate moments ■ JUDITH MORRISON, editor of *Home Entertainment,* who literally made this book a reality for me ■ PARK AVENUE AUDIO, for their sound advice and cooperation in allowing me to freely use the store's facilities ■ ARTHUR COPPOTELLI, who unselfishly promoted this book and strengthened my confidence at every opportunity ■ ALLEN SCRUGGS and DOUGLAS MYERS, Scruggs Myers & Associates, who got me started in this industry ■ TIM CLANCEY, who better learned the meaning of the word *obsession* ■ HUGO COLMAN, for the time so generously spent in poring over Jaime Ardiles-Arce's photo files ■ BRIDGET LEICESTER at Norman McGrath's studio, for the personal kindness and attention she always shows regarding my photo requests ■ And an overdue thank you to NORMAN MCGRATH for being the first photographer to work with me when I was a fledgling editor ■ PROFESSOR HARVEY ROSENBERG, who properly oriented my historical research for the book's introduction ■ FASHION INSTITUTE OF TECHNOLOGY'S LIBRARY, for use of the facility and the help of the staff ■ MARTHA KAIHATSU for showing me that there is indeed a light at the end of the tunnel—and that it is all worthwhile ■ To all the designers, audio-video consultants and installers, and the photographers—especially DAVID DERRICK and ROBIN LOVE, who managed to create beautiful photographs against all odds ■ And to ROBERT, FRANK, JAMIE, TYRONE, HENRY, CHRISSY, ANNIE, DENISE, JOAN, and DIANA, for enduring, when *my* book became *their* ordeal

CONTENTS

INTRODUCTION
PAGE 7

THE GREAT HALL
PAGE 8

THE GREAT CHAMBER
PAGE 8

LIBRARIES, GALLERIES, AND MUSIC ROOMS
PAGE 8

GREAT HALLS TO LIVING ROOMS
PAGE 10

THE FAMILY ROOM
PAGE 10

THE MODERN ERA
PAGE 11

MEDIA BASICS
PAGE 15

VIDEO COMPONENTS
PAGE 16

Component Television
Projection Television
Videocassettes vs. Videodiscs
Computer Tie-ins
Satellite Television

AUDIO COMPONENTS
PAGE 23

Digital Disc Players
The Basic Systems
Audio Accessories

PROJECT DESIGNS
PAGES 29–147

DESIGN BASICS
PAGE 149

SOUND REPRODUCTION
PAGE 150

THE LISTENING ROOM
PAGE 150

The Shape of the Room
Sound-Absorbing Decor
Soundproofing and Damping
Speaker Placement
Configuration and Mounting

COMPONENT SELECTION
PAGE 156

Discrete vs. Centralized Systems
Video Components
Audio Components

SPEAKER DESIGN
PAGE 158

Amplification and Tone Controls

OTHER DETAILS
PAGE 160

Wiring and Phasing
Lighting

THE FUTURE
PAGE 162

GLOSSARY
PAGE 164

USEFUL ADDRESSES
PAGE 166

Architects and Designers
Photographers
Audio and Video Manufacturers

BIBLIOGRAPHY
PAGE 173

INDEX
PAGE 174

Introduction

The separation of architecture from social practice is an artificial one attributable, perhaps, to the rather occluded way art history has developed in this century. Nevertheless, the two are unavoidably entwined, for architecture not only mirrors social history but responds to it as well. Social studies, however, are not restricted to mere architectural reflection; as a powerful force, an era's customs can actually mandate architectural style. Class hierarchy, domestic arrangements, sexual mores—and entertainment, in and out of the home—have all noticeably influenced the outcome of architectural planning.

Entertainment as a collective experience enjoys an ecclesiastical as well as a domestic birthright. As the epicenter of all social and cultural propriety in the Middle Ages, the church was the starting point for all medieval drama and lyric. Illustrating the fundamental ties between entertainment and architecture, the church provides a good example: masonry (rather than timber) roof vaulting was incorporated into the mainstream of Romanesque architecture solely because it enhanced the beauty of musical effects. Music in this example, provided a dramatic stimulus in the history of architectural development.

"Home entertainment" reaches far back into history, but its first noticeable effects on domestic architecture surfaced in the fourteenth century. Entertainment was regularly held indoors before the nobility and merchant bourgeoisie. In looking at entertainment's domestic birthright and its effect on interior planning, the English country house can be used as an architectural metaphor. A dwelling of the privileged class, it was also a seat of power as well as a laboratory of social change that set the standard of architecture and design. The qualities of these houses differed and so did the people who needed to be entertained and the type of entertainment they expected. Room size, function, sequence, and decoration all varied accordingly. Medieval halls, great chambers, libraries, galleries, and music rooms have all accommodated some kind of domestic entertainment since the fourteenth century and as such are all antecedents of today's media rooms and entertainment areas.

Since the beginning of the fourteenth century, music was a part of nearly all types of domestic entertainment.

The Great Hall

The old idea of a houseplan, derived from medieval times, was to provide a "great hall" for the daily use of the whole household and to supplement it with a group of rooms at each end, one for the use of the family and the other for the servants. The hall was the ceremonial as well as casual center of the home. Orchestra accompanied dinners, and banqueting processionals seemingly provided the first evidence of medieval domestic entertainment. The fanfare of music that accompanied each course remained a familiar feature of all great dinners in England well into the eighteenth century.

Indoor medieval theatrical presentations also influenced the disposition of the great hall. Staging, seating, decoration, and protocol were all modulated by the evening's entertainment. Helen Leclerc in *Les Origines italiennes de l'architecture theatrale moderne* (Paris, 1946) reiterates this idea when she suggests that the quality and very nature of a performance depend largely upon the relationship established by the actor with his audience, which in turn, is conditioned by the physical structure that contains them.

Decoration and its display was also affected. Hangings of rich tapestries enjoyed great popularity, valued as much for their warmth and better acoustical properties, which their presence afforded, as for their decorative spirit. These paintings and tapestries often represented familiar themes or stories, lending a decidedly theatrical flavor to the hall.

Insofar as our concept of the home is concerned, the time of Elizabeth I could be credited with its birth. It was in her day that the great change from medievalism took place, and houses were built for comfort and pleasure without serious thought of defense. Spaciousness, dignity, and often magnificence were the qualities aimed at in houses of the sixteenth century; most of these qualities remain appropriate in the present day.

Greater wealth and the desire for increased amenities resulted in more complex interiors, in a multiplicity of rooms in the houses of the period, including those for the common use of the family and guests—reception rooms as they would now be called.

A banquet in the Great Hall of Windsor Castle during the reign of Charles II. Guests dined on trestle tables and stools that were easily stored to make room for theatrical performances.

The Great Chamber

By the late sixteenth and early seventeenth centuries the hall had been usurped as the ceremonial pivot of the house—by the great chamber. A more intimate, private space for the lord, it was located off the hall. Although its chief function remained that of an eating place, it was far from being its only function. As the medieval taste for dancing continued to grow stronger, the great chamber was often used as an alternative venue for the performance of masques and plays as well as for games of cards, dice, or backgammon. It naturally became the most richly decorated room in the house. As a place of state, however, its fittings tended to be more permanent than those of the hall. Tables and cupboards replaced movable boards and trestle bases; chairs and stools were covered with rich fabrics. Tapestries were supplemented and sometimes replaced by pictures or carved and inlaid paneling. Quite often an elaborate plasterwork ceiling and painted frieze would be a part of the room. Although this tendency had to work against tradition, it gradually prevailed, and in so doing, radically changed the nature of the country house.

Libraries, Galleries, and Music Rooms

The sixteenth century also saw the advent of a new architectural format called the gallery. This new room tended to become a supplement or alternative to the great chamber for entertainments such as masques, games, and music.

From the sixteenth to the early eighteenth centuries, whenever people decided to entertain, they did so in much the same way. They gave either a dinner on its own or a dinner combined with dancing. The guests collectively engaged in one activity at a time.

The eighteenth century introduced more variety. Balls developed and grew larger and more elaborate. The assembly, the masquerade, the rout, the drum, the ridotto, the ridotto al fresco, and the musi-

In the beginning of the seventeenth century, "cabinets" (small rooms reserved for the owner's personal collections) were the architectural precursors of the library.

The salon of the eighteenth century usurped the earlier great hall's function as the setting for a variety of entertainments, from intimate recitals to grand balls.

By 1830 the main informal living room was usually the library. It was likely to be filled with books, comfortable furnishings, board games, and even musical instruments.

Enclosed galleries soon accommodated the sixteenth century passion for art collecting. Continuing the tradition, the walls of this sparsely furnished gallery (circa 1835) are lined with family portraits.

cal party were all new forms of entertainment which got under way at this time even though some of them had their origins in the seventeenth century.

The most important of these entertainments was the assembly. Guests met to play cards, drink tea, or walk around talking and flirting. Some assemblies, but by no means all, ended with supper. Seemingly uneventful, assemblies did, however, represent a breakthrough. They involved several activities going on at once and this made them notably less formal than earlier types of entertainment. Moreover they could easily be extended to cope with the growth of society. Assemblies of the early eighteenth century could take place in a single room; in the course of the century they tended to expand in size until they could fill half a dozen rooms or more.

As a result, the more standard axial house plan ceased to work. Instead of a hall and salon (which was formerly the great chamber), what was now needed was a series of communal rooms for entertaining, exclusive of the hall and all running into one another.

In tracing the changes that took place in the arrangement and disposition of rooms in the seventeenth and eighteenth centuries, it will be found that not much was done that made houses essentially more comfortable. Indeed, during much of this time an architect's first thought was for display and his last for comfort. Nevertheless, glorification of the individual continued to find expression in his house and his gardens. As so often happens in the case of aristocratic preoccupation, the pendulum of fashion which had swung away from art toward science, swung back again to art.

In the course of the seventeenth and eighteenth centuries, it also became more and more important for a gentleman to be cultured as well as literate. Culture became an essential part of the image of the ruling class and the country house its embodiment. Libraries, galleries, and cabinets developed to contain collections of books, maps, portraits, and other objects in great quantity.

Eventually books ceased to be the accouterments of the expert and as printing advanced, they became a part of everyday upper class life. The library and its contents were no longer the personal domain of the house's owner—they had become the common property of the family and guests. By the end of the eighteenth century libraries were essential adjuncts to the entertainment of a house party. The late

Georgian libraries were equipped with games, books, portfolios of engravings and scientific toys to amuse guests. The library had arrived as a communal living room, and in the late eighteenth and early nineteenth centuries, the country house library was at its apogee.

The basis of informal entertaining at this time was that between breakfast and dinner guests were left to a considerable extent to do what they liked. Every kind of facility was laid on for their amusement. And this in turn affected the disposition and planning of the house. Reading rooms, billiard rooms, print rooms, and even music rooms became fashionable accommodations to the leisure activities of the privileged class.

Although it may have been common for a drawing room to have a formal and an informal guise, in these larger houses informal daily life was lived in one or more other rooms. Some houses had a gallery, used for everyday living rather than just a room for pictures or dancing. But in big houses the large, informal living room was usually the library.

But on the whole, the library was reserved for quieter recreations. Music and billiards went on in other rooms—the melodies emanating from the drawing room or separate music room and the game prevailing in the billiards room or in the gallery or hall. Billiard tables had been installed in English houses since the seventeenth century but in the late eighteenth and early nineteenth centuries they became increasingly fashionable.

Everyday social life was no longer a kind of round game, in which everyone joined in together. Different people could now do different things at the same time and even in the same room. They could drift together and separate, form groups and break up in an easy and informal manner. The growing importance of the common rooms naturally affected the way rooms were decorated. In the formal house individual rooms were likely to need quick rearranging, depending on whether they were to be used for meals, cards, conversation, or dancing. Chairs were normally kept lined up along the walls and were moved into the required positions by servants. Eating tables were often folding ones, so that they could be put up and taken down with ease. When houses had a string of common rooms, each room tended to be put to a more limited set of uses. Dining rooms became rooms for eating in and nothing else; the dining room table stayed permanently in the center of the room. In the living rooms chairs and sofas remained in frozen positions suitable for conversation or in groups; lounging life encouraged softer upholstery and therefore heavier and less mobile furniture. In addition to house parties, balls and assemblies continued to take place as the numbers to be entertained increased.

Great Halls to Living Rooms

In the Victorian era, concern with morality, domesticity, organization, and hospitality remained of paramount importance. Although no new modes of entertainment were introduced, gentry and nongentry entertainments were once more being held in the same room. Called old English hospitality, these gatherings would include dances for the gentry, dinner for the tenantry or an annual summer dance. And in response to this now-fashionable custom the great hall once again reappeared—though in a vastly revised state—as the epicenter of the house's social life.

The Victorian living room, descended from the medieval great hall, remained the center of domestic entertainment.

Great halls continued to be built all through the nineteenth century and on into the twentieth century. Such halls were not necessarily modeled on medieval or Elizabethan ones but rather became more like a roofed-in courtyard with a top-lit central room. But halls of all types experienced a noticeable change in character. Although they continued to be used on occasions for balls and dinners, they also began to be used as year-round living rooms.

By the 1850s to 1860s halls often held organs, and armchairs and sofas on which house guests could listen to the music. The halls rapidly developed into comfortable living rooms, which could also be used for games, charades, and amateur theatricals. These rooms came into their own with the big house-parties. Once the rest of the house was stratified into areas for men and women, they became a useful common meeting place. Halls with staircases down into them became especially popular in the late nineteenth and early twentieth centuries, perhaps because they were nicely adapted for these evening gatherings.

Living halls remained popular but suffered from increased economies. By the 1920s living halls tended to become smaller and less exposed—and sometimes indistinguishable from ordinary rooms.

The Family Room

Soon after World War II a new addition to the American home was born: the family room. It was conceived as the place where members of the household would gather and where friends would be entertained. The baby boom had also begun, and there was a widespread feeling that houses should be designed so that parents and children could be together, unencumbered from the worries that many children created in the living room. The family room, then, became an informal place for lei-

INTRODUCTION

IN THE BEGINNING...

While the "home entertainment" industry may have begun with the invention of the phonograph in 1877, the consumer electronics industry was actually born in 1920 with the radio. Electronic home entertainment has since entered the 1980s on a technological avalanche, bringing with it a new generation of commercial products and systems. And it is this continuous stream of innovative products that continues to generate excitement—as well as a labyrinth of information. In video it centers on the emergence of component television systems, an expansion of program sources and new uses for the television screen. The newest digital high-fidelity products and improved multi-channel sound for video are also sparking a renewed interest in audio. In effect, electronic entertainment has only just begun.

surely pursuits—where togetherness could be practiced.

Electronic entertainment was just beginning to alter the patterns of leisure and home life; the result would directly affect the facilities of the family room in the 1940s and 1950s. Early radios and phonographs—usually housed in elaborate and stylized cabinets—became the new electronic "hearth," around which family members and friends would gather. Television played a major role in the change as well. In the forties and fifties television was the primary focus of domestic entertainment, preceded only by the radio. As television grew in popularity, people resisted placing the new electronic monster in their living room, preferring instead to watch it amid a more casual and unceremonious setting. When space permitted, the television was often relegated to the basement or family room, which can trace its roots back to the eighteenth-century "rustic." (In England this was generally the basement level of a house where the servants were quartered along with one or more informal family rooms.) Reinterpreted in the fifties, it became a space for casual family gatherings, hobbies, games, listening to music, and watching television.

Advances in high fidelity made music an integral part of life, too. The record player, radio, and tape recorder joined the television as electronic marvels of the fifties. The advent of more equipment aroused a desire for new, sophisticated integration techniques. Sound walls became a popular design vehicle of the day. Before long even the jukebox made its way into those more progressive homes as a novel piece of entertainment to supplement the existing music system.

The Modern Era

By the 1960s a new attitude took effect, whereby component design was creating a specific image. Home entertainment equipment was sleeker and began to acquire an array of lights, dials, toggle switches, and slide controls that more closely resembled the cockpit of a spaceship. Elaborate equipment became a new status symbol, emblematic of money and leisure. Still not much had been accomplished regarding the integration of an entire system. The most imaginative solutions simply placed the equipment on shelves or hid them behind cabinet doors.

The late sixties and early seventies saw a rise in home entertaining, as more fully integrated audio and video systems became available to the consumer. New terminology such as "entertainment room" had greater social implications and shifted emphasis away from the family. For the apartment dweller this more likely translated into an entertainment "section," which was incorporated into an existing room. Such is the beginning of the multipurpose room.

The inflationary climate of the seventies and eighties saw the birth of an unchecked real estate spiral in which space became a most precious commodity. A shaky economy kept even more people at home, entertaining there rather than going out for an evening's amusement. Consequently, new attention was given to home electronics—not merely as functional objects but also as sources of pleasure and even culture. But this did not happen overnight. Recent technology has produced new program sources making television more a vehicle of personal choice than a puppet of network programming. Videodiscs and personal computers have now introduced the opportunity for human interactivity just as new kinds of electronics will undoubtedly continue to expand the limits of entertainment, education, and information services. The architectural and design ramifications can be seen in the development of the integrated home-entertainment system.

Media rooms used for the exclusive purpose of audio-video entertainment share a new compatibility with the components themselves. The architecture, lighting, seating, wiring, and placement of equipment is geared for acoustic as well as visual aesthetics. As these considerations grow in importance, electronic integration will reach a new level of sophistication within the home. The self-contained media system—where all the components are assembled together on one wall—is more common in rooms where a multifunctional capability is required. Nevertheless, one room can now function as a film library, screening room, game room, and work station without sacrificing the design integrity.

Shaping an entertainment system in the 1980s requires the application of new planning principles tempered by the special needs of the electronic technology at hand. More specifically, the architecture, furnishings, and even the client's expectations must be carefully orchestrated in light of new technological parameters.

For the design community this is an extraordinary challenge. The ground rules are changing, and these changes require special considerations. First and foremost is the need to become educated about the new technology—how it will affect the way rooms work and what the environmental requirements of the equipment are. Most important is a knowledgeable application of the criteria and considerations that are unique to the components themselves.

MEDIA DESIGN

In 1939 RCA introduced this Art Deco-inspired console with built-in television and radio; it sold for $450.

RCA showed their first mass-produced black-and-white television set in 1946.

In 1941 Philco produced this stylish radio/phonograph combination with its unique "drop-front" speaker

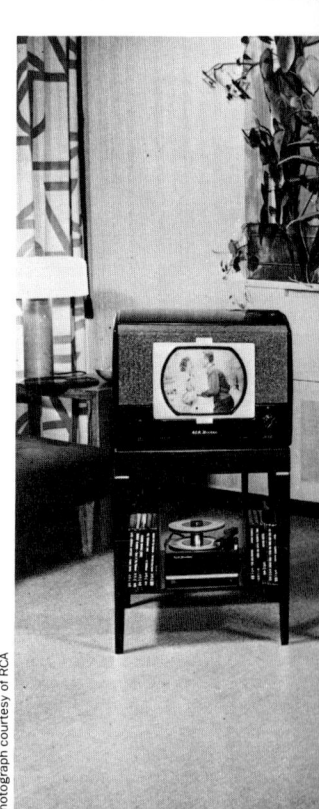

INTRODUCTION

The first all-electronic compatible color television system was introduced circa 1951; shown is RCA's 21-inch prototype.

As Americans became increasingly style-conscious, RCA offered a selection of three tabletop models, in 1950.

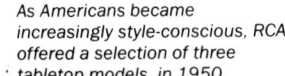

By the late 60s, the move toward contemporary interior design saw the introduction of this console television with molded white cabinet and rosewood veneer (Ransgate GT-803 from RCA).

Media Basics

Electronic media equipment for home entertainment is currently experiencing a unique renaissance. No longer eclipsed by outmoded social prejudices or poor design, audio-video systems have become the new centerpiece of home entertainment. Before attempting to incorporate such components into a domestic architectural scheme, a general overview of the hardware itself—its function and design—is the logical first step in determining your needs.

MEDIA / DESIGN

Video Components

Television is still the major component of home entertainment. New uses and requirements are undoubtedly contributing to an accelerated demand and with it a new wave of design modifications to enhance both its appearance and ease of operation. The television screen has suddenly become an all-purpose display device, a separate entity from the broadcast. Video games now let viewers interact with their screens for the first time. Videocassette recorders (VCRs) permit viewers to rearrange timed broadcasts to suit their own schedules and permit them to develop their own programming. Along with VCRs, videodisc players increase program choices, augment "realtime" broadcast and cable transmissions, and add a new entertainment dimension through stereo sound. Home computers utilize the same home display center, and videotex systems permit interaction with computers outside the home.

■ COMPONENT TELEVISION

Since the introduction of color television in 1954, and prior to the most recent developments, there have been few milestones in home television. By design, the conventional television quality of performance and flexibility have been sacrificed to fit the entire system into a single cabinet. As electronic sophistication and program sources proliferated, television's unfulfilled potential became evident; its evolution into component television was a natural course of events. **Component television** simply separates a conventional television into its basic parts: the display screen (monitor); the receiver section (tuner), including broadcast and cable tuners, videocassette recorders, and videodiscs; and the speaker system. Dividing the single television set into separate packages allows each unit to reach its state-of-the-art performance. The result is an interactive, high quality audio and video system.

Pioneer's Foresight 7000 entertainment system features component video and audio housed on a brushed aluminum trolley.

A **monitor** is simply a picture tube and its associated circuits—it is not a self-contained television set and is therefore useless without a program source or tuner. As a rule monitors feature high-definition picture tubes, video/audio inputs and outputs, digital video input for direct home-computer connection, and a two-channel internal audio system. In component video systems, the monitor and the tuner can be separate components; the tuner can also be built into the monitor, in which case it is called a monitor/receiver. Such monitor/receivers are complete television sets that have provisions for external audio amplifiers, speakers, etc. and are designed to accept videocassette recorders, videodiscs, and other program sources on a plug-in basis.

Selecting the right video monitor is crucial to the success and enjoyment of your system. Accurate image reproduction is the keynote here. Evaluating the performance of a conventional television set or monitor is not a complicated process. The final picture quality depends on several easy-to-see characteristics: overscan, black level, linearity, and convergence and detail.

Overscan refers to that "cropped" portion of the television image that you can't see. Cropped on all sides of the screen, overscan can represent as much as twenty percent of the original picture. To compare systems for overscan look at all four edges of the screen. Any program with an extreme close-up will yield a clear indication of a system's ability to keep up with constantly changing requirements. Watch for how much the picture itself shrinks and expands.

Before the monitor can deliver a fine color picture, it needs to create an accurate black-and-white image. An exceptionally stable power supply is required to produce a black black without sacrificing the brilliance of the whites or the details in the darker portions of the picture. It is an important consideration since black affects not only color reproduction but depth of field as well. To judge a system's *black-level* ability, select an image that contains both black and white. An ineffective monitor will show dark gray rather than black. Whites may be gray and details are relatively lost.

Another important consideration in evaluating a video monitor is the ability to

MEDIA BASICS

FROM TELEVISION TO VIDEO

The most significant movement in home entertainment media can be summed up in one word—video. At the fulcrum of an electronics revolution, video is changing our basic sources of entertainment, information, education, and communication. Consider, for example, the transformation from television to video. For many years, the conventional television set served one purpose—the reception and reproduction of broadcast programs. Community antenna television (CATV) systems, which augmented the choice of broadcasts and improved reception, evolved into today's cable television, which now can provide up to one hundred channels or more of entertainment, information, and service. Television is becoming less of a passive instrument. Premium service or pay television was added to cable. Similar services, including broadcast subscription television and microwave-delivered MDS TV, were added in areas where cable had not penetrated. Other new program sources have begun to proliferate.

Proton's 600 M color video monitor features an all-black housing with 19-inch diagonally measured picture.

reproduce the actual shape and colors of an object. The accuracy of shape is most obvious when the picture has a straight line—the straighter the line the better the system's geometric *linearity* and the more accurate all images will be shaped. To judge a monitor's geometric linearity it is easiest to use the lines on a field or court of a sports broadcast. The more curved or bent the lines appear, the more other images will be distorted as well.

Poor *convergence* shows up as color fringes around the edges of an image and with overall inaccurate color. It is easiest to test convergence with a black-and-white broadcast on your color set. In a color monitor black-and-white images are actually reproduced by combining red, green, and blue light. If the system has good convergence, the colors are combined accurately and you will see nothing but black, white, and gray. Good convergence is necessary to produce sharp images and accurate color.

A monitor's ability to reproduce *detail* is of obvious importance, and almost any noise-free program (see Glossary) can be used to evaluate it. Small graphics or patterns in a picture such as in clothing, facial hair, or backgrounds may be used. Two characteristics of the monitor have a major effect on its ability to reproduce fine details. The first is the size of the picture tube's phosphor dot spots, which are illuminated to create the picture. The smaller the size of the spot, more spots can be positioned on a line and the greater the detail can be. The second characteristic contributing to picture detail is the monitor's video frequency response. This measures how often the electron (monitor's) beam can be turned on and off during each scan across the screen or how many phosphor dots it can illuminate. The higher the frequency, the more detailed the picture can be. Most televisions have a frequency response ranging from 58 MHz to 1025 MHz. Compare the information on different manufacturer's specifications. You can determine the upper limits of a monitor's resolution by multiplying the monitor's frequency response by 80. Yields of 330 horizontal lines of resolution from a television signal and 400 lines from a direct video input are excellent.

Most commonly in a video component system the **broadcast tuner** is designed as only one of several plug-in program sources. The monitor, as already mentioned, is equipped with direct *video inputs,* providing for direct hookup to a videocassette recorder or videodisc player. Using the tuner section of an attached VCR allows for a complete TV/VCR system with better television reception and better VCR playback quality than a conventional television setup. A tuner may also have a *video output,* which can accommodate an additional monitor for simultaneous yet independent viewing without signal degradation or impedance matching problems (see Glossary). An unusual feature available on more complex monitors is a *digital color video input,* allowing for the direct connection to a personal computer for alphanumeric or color graphics. Lastly, an *audio input* enables you to hook up speakers to the monitor so viewers can hear the broadcast in stereo.

As the nerve center of the entire video component system, the tuner acts as an extremely sophisticated routing and switching network that integrates the entire system, in some cases by remote control. Equipped with its own complete set of inputs/outputs, a separate tuner allows for maximum flexibility within the framework of current technology. Tuners generally match the monitor's styling and look much like an audio component. Most set-ups place the tuner near the monitor, either just above or below it.

Some special features to look for are *automatic switching* (to a new program source), *dual video outputs* (with one output delivering the main program to the primary viewing monitor while the other output directs the VCR, compact disc player, or television signal to a secondary monitor or to another VCR for dubbing), and *dual antenna inputs* (for the connection of cable service to antenna A and a satellite dish to antenna B).

The metamorphosis from television to video is reemphasizing an often neglected link in the television chain—audio. Television broadcasting, as well as cable, videodiscs, and other program sources, now places new emphasis on high-fidelity audio, and set manufacturers have vastly improved their products' sound capabilities to take advantage of this new dimension. The television set's speaker systems are improved in graduated levels of sophistication. Some sets include two-channel audio for stereo VCR/videodisc playback and audio-expansion circuitry to add much of the enjoyment of true stereo listening to standard television broadcasts or monaural videocassettes. Many "high end" models include separate balance, bass/treble controls, or an integrated FM tuner (stereo) for simulcast television shows or FM listening. Selected sets also include expanded speaker systems with woofers and tweeters. Increasingly, television sets are incorporating audio output jacks for the integration of home high fidelity components into the viewing/listening chain.

One of the most important trends from the recent past has been **wireless remote control.** Purely a convenience device, remote control (generally no bigger than a hand-held calculator) offers viewers complete operational functions from across the room. These include channel select, volume control, on-off, a panel lock button to lock out controls at the set. Some may even be able to tune in cable stations. With

RCA's Digital Command Center is a full-function, wireless remote control unit. The dark Plexiglas panel, on the left, lifts open to reveal additional switches.

the spread of multi-channel cable television systems, most manufacturers offer color sets that are "cable ready" or capable of tuning special cable channels without the use of an external converter. An advisable aesthetic consideration, this development also makes it possible to use the television's remote control features with cable systems.

■ PROJECTION TELEVISION

Giant-screen projection color television has been fully integrated into the video product spectrum. Virtually every major manufacturer features at least one model. Although still relatively new, modern design and styling have made these systems an aesthetic addition to the home. Technological advances in picture definition and brightness aside, a new generation of more compact rear projection units is expected to further increase the popularity of giant-screen television.

The principle behind projection television is deceptively simple. A picture tube is fitted with a special lens (three lenses in the more sophisticated models) to focus the projected image on a special screen, set at a prescribed distance. The relationship of projector to screen is directly proportional: the closer the screen, the smaller the image; the farther the screen, the larger the image. There are currently three major types of projection television with screen sizes ranging from forty feet to more than six feet in diagonal measurement: 1) the two-piece front projection unit, with separate screens and projector/receivers; 2) a one-piece front projection system, incorporating the screen and projector in a fold-out or hinged drawer; and 3) a single-piece rear projection unit, incorporating a translucent screen to display the picture projected from inside the cabinet.

Most experts currently agree that front projection sets display the best picture but usually take up more space. In the *one-piece front projection* unit, the projector at the base of the screen projects the image at a mirror which then reflects it onto the screen. When the set is operational, the drawer containing the projector must remain fully open. In a *two-piece front projection* system, the projector and screen are separate components. The projector is usually placed in an unobstructed line of vision a specified number of feet from the screen. Some models are available with ceiling mounted projectors, which save space, or with projectors that can be disguised as coffee tables. The *rear projection* system is smaller than the other two, but the quality of the picture generally is not as good.

Some projection television sets incorporate a *single-tube system* much like the television tube in a conventional monitor, which loses brightness as it travels to the projection screen. This system delivers a somewhat inferior picture, which is best watched in a totally darkened room. *Three-tube systems* are acknowledged to offer the best performance. The three-tube projector incorporates three high-output cathode ray tubes (CRTs), which project red, blue, and green elements through three separate lenses. These primary colors pass through the lens assembly and converge on the screen to form an image. Optical glass and special nonreflective coatings ensure optimum image transfer and eliminate discoloration.

Read the specifications for each screen unit. The f-stop rating on the lens assembly will help you evaluate the available three-tube systems. The f-stop measures the aperture of the lens assembly and

Designed with smaller spaces in mind, the one-piece front projection TV (left) and rear projection TV (right) are from NEC.

therefore indicates how much light can pass through. The more light, the brighter the picture; the smaller the f-stop number, the wider the lens aperture. So, the smaller f-stop numbers provide the brighter pictures. The screen itself will also affect the image's brightness. The newest screens are specially treated to resist dust and to eliminate deterioration and allow cleaning.

Specifications are also useful in evaluating the quality of the screen. The gain figure, for example, measures how much brighter a screen is as opposed to the projected image against a flat, white wall. The viewing angle—the plus- or minus-figure—indicates how much of an angle from the center you can move and still see an image half as bright. A higher figure ensures a greater angle at which you can watch your projection television and still see a bright image. This figure is especially useful in planning your seating configuration and overall room arrangement.

The better projection sets accommodate audio-video flexibility in much the same way as separate video components. Wireless remote can allow direct access to 105 channels (including the 23 cable channels) from across the room as well as power on-off, station scan, volume mute, and lock. Separate audio and video inputs can accommodate a VCR or videodisc player, eliminating the need for accessory switchboxes and cables. Direct connection (rather than via a radio-frequency connector) of the VCR or videodisc player yields a picture with far less "noise" or electronic interference. Audio input plugs allow the option of interfacing with a stereo system and thereby listening to selected broadcasts in stereo (network television is not broadcast in stereo, but many videotapes, videodiscs, and some cable shows are). Select models may have separate bass, treble, and balance controls and even a built-in stereo tuner for simulcast television shows or FM listening.

■VIDEOCASSETTES VS. VIDEODISCS

The first new major video program source for the television receiver since the advent of cable television is the **videocassette** recorder (VCR). The development of the VCR is a natural extension of videotape, the standard medium in television programming. Used because of low production costs—instant and unlimited playback of recorded material, cheap and fast editing—videotape not only changed the

DESIGN

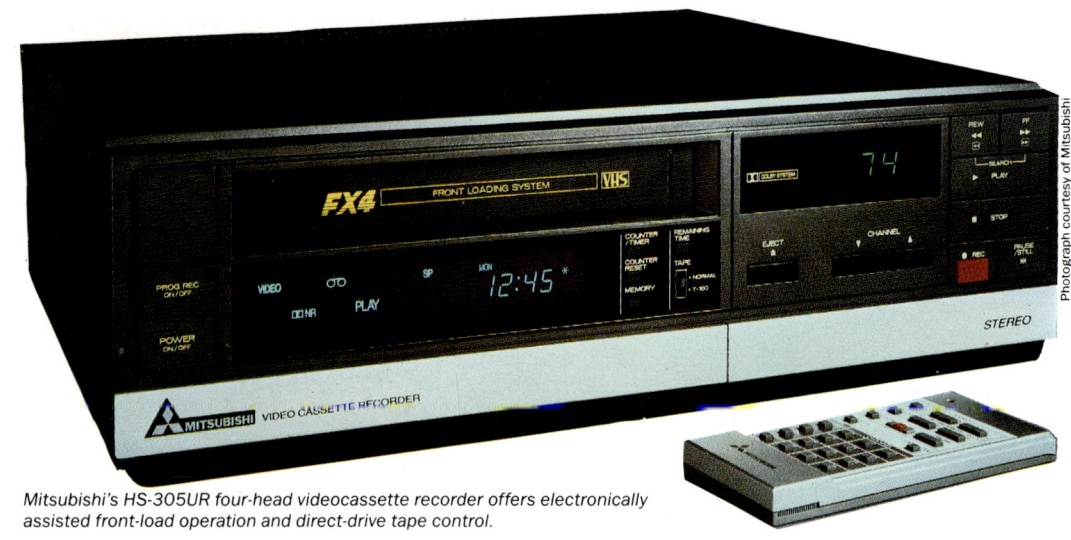

Mitsubishi's HS-305UR four-head videocassette recorder offers electronically assisted front-load operation and direct-drive tape control.

VCR: A CLOSER LOOK
Following is a list of features common to both systems:

Multiple speeds—Most decks can be set to run at two or three different speeds. At slower speeds, recording time is extended up to three or six hours with standard videocassette tape and five to eight hours with thinner tape. Faster speeds are included because they yield a superior picture and sound quality, although the picture quality at even the slowest speeds has been judged more than acceptable.

Picture search and scan—This feature allows the user to go through the tape at high speed while the picture remains visible. It makes the prospect of searching for a particular section of tape not only feasible but convenient as well. Interference lines may occur on the screen, but these will not curtail the search and scan capabilities.

Tuners/timers—All home VCRs except portables have built-in tuners/timers. This allows the machine to record any available station at a preselected time, operating much the same way as the clock in a clock radio. The reduced size and weight of the battery-operated portable VCRs is possible due to the use of a separate tuner/timer. The tuner/timer has a power supply to recharge the portable's battery and to run the deck on regular AC power when used indoors.

Programmable tuner/timers—More sophisticated than their standard counterparts, these allow the recording of several different programs at different times on different channels. The machine can be set from one day to two weeks or more in advance to automatically record up to capacity.

---

television industry but also introduced a new dimension to home entertainment.

Physically resembling an audio component, videocassette recorders play and record sight-and-sound tapes through a television set or monitor. Using half-inch tape in easy-to-load cassettes, VCRs can record "programs" from both network and cable channels or from cameras. Prerecorded videocassettes of popular movies and music videos are currently enjoying phenomenal success. Equipped with timer, the VCR affords the luxury of flexibility in time scheduling. The simplest timer, for example, allows for preset recording of a single program at a given time, while the more sophisticated timers permit preset programming of up to eight programs on eight different channels. Home components range from basic units to models with special effects such as freeze frame, variable slow and fast motion, visible forward and reverse scan, wireless remote control of all functions, and even stereo recording and playback capability.

There are two incompatible VCR formats to consider: the *Beta* and the *VHS* (Video Home System). While performance differences between the two formats is negligible, there are technical distinctions. The way the tape threads around the heads differs: The Beta wrap resembles a sideways "U," while the VHS wrap resembles the letter "M." Although both formats use half-inch tape and both housings are one-inch thick, the cassettes themselves are slightly different. (The Beta cassette measures approximately 4" x 6¼" and the VHS cassette is about 4" x 7½".) The cassettes are not interchangeable.

Tape speeds vary between the two formats. The VHS system has three speeds, which play at one time the normal speed, two times the normal speed, and three times the normal speed. The speeds are labeled for easy differentiation: SP, LP, and SLP, respectively. Take a 120-minute cassette, for example. At SP the cassette will run for two hours; at LP it will run for four hours; and at SLP it will play or record for six hours. The Beta format also has three speeds: x1, x2, and x3. At the x1 speed, you can record or play for two hours on a 120-minute cassette. The x2 speed will record or play for approximately three hours and twenty minutes on the same cassette, while the x3 runs on the same cassette for approximately five hours. The latter is labeled "L830."

Three types of VCR designs appear in both the Beta and VHS format. The *basic tabletop VCR* records and plays tapes at all speeds and can be preprogrammed within a twenty-four-hour period. A *full-feature tabletop VCR* has the same tape speed capacity, can be preprogrammed beyond a twenty-four-hour period, and permits still frames, fast scans, and slow-motion viewing. The *portable VCR* and tuner/timer, with the same tape capacity as the others, may allow for special effects depending on the manufacturer and permits recording and playback anywhere. All have a battery operation option.

A new videocassette format, which uses only quarter-inch-wide tape, is expected to be on the market in 1984. Featured in miniature portable VCRs and portable camera-recorder (camcorder) combinations, the new format will have a maximum play time of two hours per cassette. This means that the longer-playing half-inch videocassettes (up to eight hours) will be the standard for in-home use.

Despite early growing pains and reports of unrealized expectations, it is the **videodisc** system that has stretched entertainment to new limits. Similar in function to the phonograph, the videodisc player plays sight-and-sound discs through a television set or monitor. Unlike the VCR, the videodisc player is a playback-only device and cannot be used to record. Deceptively simple to operate, videodiscs are designed to be a relatively low-cost, high-quality video entertainment medium. There are currently three mutually incompatible videodisc systems on the market: the grooved *CED (Capacitance Electronic Disc),* the grooveless optical *LV (LaserVision),* and the grooveless *VHD (Video High Density)* system introduced in Japan. Of the three systems, the LV and VHD offer the greatest number of features at a slightly higher price.

Both the CED and VHD use plastic discs stamped into the shape of a record and measuring about twelve inches in diameter. They are stored in a permanent caddy, so the disc itself is never touched. An internal stylus reads the peaks and valleys on the disc's surface by electronic sensing. Different from the conventional stylus on a turntable which actually rides in the grooves, the stylus of the CED videodisc actually rides just above them. The readings are then translated into audio, video, and radio frequency signals sent to the television set or monitor.

The LV system is truly remarkable and therefore demands more explanation. Rather than using a microscopic diamond stylus, the LV utilizes a laser beam mounted on the base of the player. When aimed at the disc, the beam discerns the information stored in tiny pits (not grooves) on the surface, translating the stored information into a television picture, sound, and data. The laserdiscs also differ from the plastic discs used by the other formats. They are silver with a clear acrylic coating and measure about the same size as a

The Pioneer LaserDisc (Laser Diode Tracer Front Loading System) features brushed aluminum housing and a wireless remote control unit.

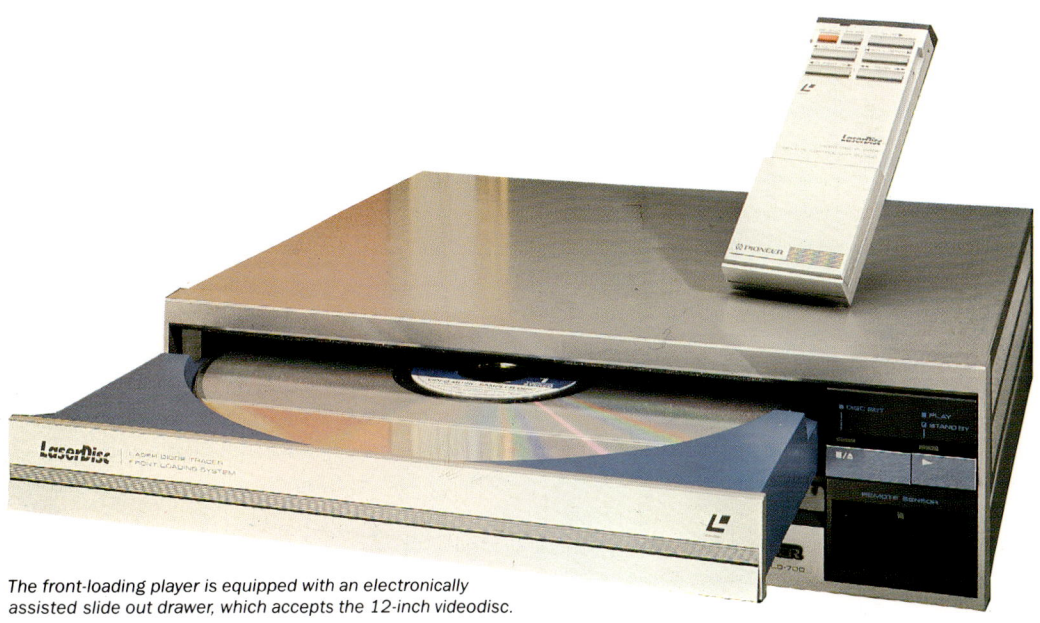

The front-loading player is equipped with an electronically assisted slide out drawer, which accepts the 12-inch videodisc.

MEDIA DESIGN

The Kaypro home computer has an adjustable CRT display and a separate keyboard.

conventional long-playing phonograph record. There is no protective caddy.

Two kinds of laserdiscs are produced—CAV (Constant Angular Velocity) or CLV (Constant Linear Velocity)—both of which play from the center to the edge. With thirty minutes on each side, CAV discs spin at a constant speed of 1800 revolutions per minute, which allows for various special effects (see box on VCR Features). CLV discs run sixty minutes per side in an extended-play mode. The speed of the CLV disc varies from 1800 revolutions per minute at the center to 600 revolutions per minute at the outside rim. The CAV discs have the capability for special interactive programming; the CLV discs do not.

Interactive or **participative programs** take advantage of the freeze frame, random access, and chapter search capabilities of the system. Programs such as these can be stored and recalled for repeated viewing and participation. In addition, they have no running time. More than a dozen interactive discs are now available for use on LV players.

Games on videodiscs are not the same as video games. The graphics are not limited to computer graphics. The LV screen can show live actors or sophisticated animation, and the sound is the same as television sound.

Again, there are basic differences between the two most popular program sources—the VCR and the videodisc. The simple and most important difference is that disc systems provide playback only whereas videocassettes have both playback and recording capabilities. Second, the interactive options offered by some videodisc systems remains beyond the technology of videotape. In addition, the cost of a videodisc now runs about $20 for an entire motion picture as opposed to $50 to $75 for a prerecorded videocassette. You should be cognizant that available programming is increasing rapidly. Several dozen new releases are added monthly. Disc owners no longer have to wait for a recent movie to be released on disc long after the videocassette release. Simultaneous cassette and disc release should be a reality in the very near future. Furthermore, nearly every major home-video programming manufacturer has released a substantial portion of its videocassette library on both videodisc formats.

■ COMPUTER TIE-INS

Though personal **home computers** have been available for the past nine years, 1983 marked the year of ultimate computer consciousness. The programmable video game blazed the trail for the computer. For many people, games offered the first look at the practical applications of the computer, demonstrated the graphics and information handling capabilities, and showed how the machines work under the control and orders of the user.

The console or keyboard is the command center of any personal computer. To activate the "brains" of video games and computers accurately programmed instructions, or software, is needed. Preprogrammed software is available commercially as plug-in cartridges or on magnetic cassette tapes or discs. The continuous introduction of new entertainment, educational, and home management programs has helped fuel the computer market. Owners recognized their computers as tools capable of educating, word processing, managing financial matters, and electronic filing.

Computers are also beginning to appear

COMPUTER BITS

The first fully digital computer built in the United States dates back only to World War II. Unveiled at the University of Pennsylvania in 1946 the 30-ton monster was christened ENIAC for Electronic Numerical Integrator and Calculator. A collection of 18,000 vacuum tubes, 7,000 resistors, 10,000 capacitors, and 6,000 switches, ENIAC occupied the space of a two-car garage. Scientific advances, however, rapidly changed the physical demeanor of the computer. The transistor and the miniaturized circuit in the 1950s reduced the workings of a room size computer to a tiny silicon chip. Developing alongside these design advances are new user trends that have greatly expanded the electronic brain industry. Within the past decade applications of electronic technology have spread from the manufacturing and accounting sectors of corporate operations into the daily routine of the home.

within the array of state-of-the-art video components. Although the newest video game console systems include a built-in video display, a television set or special monitor delivers the best picture. Large screen projection television can bring video game images to life in a way that smaller screens can't even approach.

For practical purposes consider the monitor (with either integrated or separate video tuner) as a display for conventional and cable television programming, videotapes, and videodiscs. If equipped with an RGB input (Red-Green-Blue color information signal) the home computer can be fed directly into the tuner and use the monitor for textual and graphic information generated by the computer. A 14-inch monitor will provide comfortable use, while a 19-inch monitor will be more comfortable for group viewing. One will also want to ensure that the keyboard is placed at a comfortable distance from the screen, allowing the user to comfortably see the goings on.

As software continues to become more "user friendly" (earlier to use and understand and implement), skeptics will become more curious and will begin to understand how useful computers can be. Software is currently divided into such categories as entertainment, education, home business, and utility.

As the home computer gains acceptance and increases in its penetration of households across the country, the concept of electronic delivery of information and entertainment software gains currency. It is not a dream or a service to be enjoyed by a few. Rather, it is on the verge of becoming a mass-consumer service. Of course the personal computer is already a machine with formidable capabilities. Yet those capabilities can be multiplied almost indefinitely by plugging into a network of other computers. Called telecommunicating, it can generally be done with a small device, which attaches to the phone, called a **modem**. One can then send electronic mail across the country or access information data banks. What the telephone can't deliver because of data capacity limitations, the cable systems will be able to augment if not completely replace.

The Sony CDP-101 digital disc player, with a matte black finish and a front-loading platter, automatically loads and cues the disc at the touch of a button.

Various information systems using the home television screen are now undergoing trials in many parts of the country. Known by the generic term *videotex*, the two major systems are **Teletext** and **Viewdata**. Teletext may be transmitted by television stations and cable systems simultaneously with television programs and can provide a wide variety of text and graphic material—constantly updated data such as sports scores, stock market reports, airline schedules, movie and concert listings, traffic conditions, etc.—which viewers can call onto the screen at will. Viewdata is a two-way service that can use telephone or cable television lines to provide homes with access to computer data from many sources. A true home readout system connected to a large number of central computers, Viewdata provides many types of service from remote library searches to electronic banking and electronic mail. Both of these systems, when interfaced to the home television set or video component system, expand home video far beyond its entertainment functions into an area of "information utility."

■ SATELLITE TELEVISION

Also available is the home satellite earth station for direct reception of programs intended primarily for use by television stations and cable systems. These TVRO (TV Receive-Only) stations, while still expensive, are gradually declining in price, and are most popular in remote rural areas where there is limited access to cable and multi-channel broadcasting. Future stations should bring direct broadcasting from satellites to homes on special frequencies that permit smaller antennas and simpler home reception gear. These advances will expand the home satellite business and provide major new sources of programs—perhaps in a new wide-screen, high-definition form, which once again would revolutionize the revolutionary business of video.

Audio Components

The audio industry has been poised for several years on the threshold of its own revolution with the advent of digital technology. Rapid advances in the use of microprocessors—computers on a chip—have already signaled a radical departure in the recording and reproduction of high-fidelity sound. Designed to interface with an existing component stereo system, **digital disc players** and **digital audio discs (DAD)** entered the market for the first time in 1983.

DESIGN

■ DIGITAL DISC PLAYERS

The player is typically less than one half the size of a turntable and uses a laser beam to read information stored on the surface of a reflective disc. Measuring just four and three-quarters of an inch in diameter, the discs resemble small records and hold up to one hour of music. Dubbed the **Compact Disc (CD)** system, its profound contribution to audiotechnology is virtually distortion-free sound. There is no background noise, no flutter, and no tape hiss; the dynamic range is higher than it has ever been on any home system before.

Digital processing represents both the future and the end of the long quest for the perfect method of sound recording and playback. Ever since Thomas Edison's first talking machine, sound reproduction has been based on an analog principle: The sound source (record, tape, or radio broadcast) has been a physical or electrical representation of the original musical wave form. This in turn was translated into "patterns" formed in the grooves of phonograph record masters or in the oxide particles of master tapes. Playback was subsequently accomplished by either one of two ways: the back-and-forth motion of a phono cartridge or by variations in a magnetic signal recorded on tape.

The analog system is better in theory than in practice. Its main disadvantage is that imperfections in the recording medium inevitably show up in the recorded music. Although noise reduction devices are used to cover some of the sonic problems, all of these systems invariably introduce their own set of problems. Add to this the fact that a high-quality vinyl for record-making cannot be used in the United States due to governmental restrictions, the result is warped records, clicks, pops, ticks, and poor tracking.

Rather than trying to reproduce a complex audio wave form, digital recording converts the music to a binary digital code. Translated into on-and-off pulses called bits, the code is stored on the disc surface and protected with plastic coating. On playback the pulses are tracked by a laser beam and converted back into an analog signal and then into sound. Since a digital recording consists of on-and-off pulses, there is no way that imperfections in the recording medium—whether it is a tape or disc—can affect the sound. Since there are no limitations in dynamic range, loud passages are distortion-free and quiet passages are totally silent. Once inserted in the player, the DAD spins like an LP disc but much faster. Instead of flipping the DAD over to hear the second side (like an LP record), you can program the DAD to play songs in any order or to repeat. Since it uses a laser instead of a stylus it is not subject to groove wear, warps, dirt, dust, and fingerprints. A final advantage in digital recording is that digital tapes and discs can be copied over and over again without degradation in sound quality.

A "LIVE" ROOM

Reverberation time and forced vibration are functions of listening-room size and of the relationship of absorbent to reflective materials used. When a sound starts in a room, for example, it does not reach maximum intensity immediately (and conversely when it is stopped, the intensity does not immediately collapse to zero). The time it takes to build up and collapse is a function of the total absorbency and hence reflectivity and room volume. These effects stem from the echoes from the reflecting surfaces. The time it takes after the source has stopped for the sound to fall by one millionth of the original energy is known as the reverberation time.

A greater reverberation time constitutes a live room with a greater degree of coloration, while a lesser reverberation time constitutes a dead room, approaching anechoic chamber. The reverberation time of a concert hall or church may be several seconds. The reverberant coloration of a live room is required, because it constitutes part of the signal information that is responsible for the acoustic atmosphere of the reproduction. If the reverberation time of the listening room is too great, however, the definition of the reproduction can be impaired. So for the best high-fidelity reproduction, you must construct a live room that maintains a balance of absorptive and reflective qualities to ensure sonic integrity without reverberation in keeping with the listening preference of the user.

■ THE BASIC SYSTEMS

Still considered the building block of even the most basic home entertainment system, stereos are currently available in three formats: the "compact," an all-in-one table model consisting of a turntable mounted in a cabinet with tuner/amplifier, and optional cassette or cartridge facilities; the "one brand" or "uni-brand" system consisting of separate components matched by the manufacturer or the dealer; and the independent component system whereby the owner or listener selects the range of components.

The **compact system** has been the mainstay of the industry for the past twenty years, offering inexpensive units that are operationally simple. Their sound is generally considered inferior to that of a separate component system and is therefore not recommended as a primary system. An alternative is the **one-brand system** for those who want component-quality audio without having to match up components made by different companies. Most come complete with a special cabinet. These systems are traditionally easy to install and operate, and they produce far better sound than compact systems.

Two other types of all-in-one or uni-brand systems have recently gathered a good deal of popular acceptance. The first is the **micro component system,** made up of units about half the size of conventional audio components. Although small, such systems provide the full complement of features offered by the traditional-size components. The important difference is that the amplifier power outputs are smaller than regular-size amplifiers. The micro series are especially appealing to those with limited space for equipment or for those who want audio equipment to be minimally visible in their decor.

The other all-in-one system format is the **midi system,** made up of components sized between traditional models and the micro units. These systems satisfy those listeners who are looking for smaller equipment with enough mass to satisfy the "bigger is better" syndrome. This system also

MEDIA BASICS

Nakamichi Dragon-CT Computing Turntable

Nakamichi RX-202 Unidirectional Auto Reverse Cassette Deck

Luxman LX104 Duo-Beta DC Integrated Stereo Amplifier

Sony Audio Current Transfer FM Stereo Tuner ST-S555ES

Luxman RX-103 90-Watt/Channel Digital Synthesized Receiver

B&W DM110 Loudspeakers

25

DESIGN

> **EIGENTONES**
>
> There is bound to be some to-and-fro bouncing of the sound waves between room surfaces and hence some reverberation. At certain frequencies, the reflections can precipitate a "standing-wave resonance" or eigentone. When the half wavelength of a sound wave corresponds to the distance between two walls, an eigentone is established. Because the sound pressure rises at the boundaries of the room relative to the middle-lower pressure area, a listener moving in the sound field will experience changes in loudness of the particular frequency. Eigentones can also occur when the reflecting surfaces are placed to coincide with a measurement of a multiple of the sound half the wavelength.
>
> The trouble can become more severe if the room is a cube, in which eigentones coincide in all dimensions; the pressure build-up at certain locations in the room then becomes significant and makes a poor room for listening.

provides higher amplifier power outputs than the micro.

Independent components still offer the best sound quality and versatility. They allow you to assemble a personalized system. This choice also permits a logical and systematic method of upgrading; as technological advances take place or as personal taste becomes more demanding, the system can be improved piece by piece.

All basic stereo component systems are composed of three types of components: **the signal sources, the receiver, and the speakers.** Signal sources provide the audio signals that are amplified and processed by the rest of the system. A turntable, tuner, tape deck, and compact disc player are the most common signal sources. A **turntable** plays records by way of a cartridge held by a tonearm which tracks a disc (record). The output voltage of a turntable is very low, requiring amplification as well as equalization. Providing signal sources at higher levels, the **compact disc player** plays a DAD by means of a laser, the **tape deck** records and plays back cassette tapes, and a **tuner** picks up AM and FM radio signals.

A **receiver** precludes the need for a separate tuner and instead performs the triple functions of the tuner, the preamplifier (or control amplifier), and the power amplifier. The *preamplifier* section contains the basic switching and sound processing controls; its main function is to amplify the cartridge output of a turntable. The preamp also permits tone control with bass and treble controls, balance between two stereo channels, volume, and signal source selection. The *power amplifier* section makes the signal powerful enough to drive the speakers.

Loudspeakers actually produce sound by turning electrical power into vibrations of a diaphragm—usually a cone or a dome. Drivers are the various cones and domes that make up a speaker and an enclosure is the box that contains them. A basic speaker will have two drivers: a *woofer* for the low sounds and a *tweeter* for the high sounds. A three-way system includes a separate midrange driver. An electrical circuit in the loudspeaker called a crossover splits the incoming signal into the high and low frequency parts sending them to the tweeter and woofer respectively.

Following the lead of the compact disc manufacturers, speaker companies are now producing "digital ready" speakers. If you are considering the addition of a digital audio signal source such as a compact disc, also consider investing in these speakers. Whether or not a speaker is capable of producing digital music depends on its own dynamic range—the difference between its loudest and softest extremes—and on the power available from the power amplifier. A most delicate situation arises when you want to add a digital player to an existing traditional system. In determining whether the whole system will work without damaging any of its parts, you will have to be cognizant of decibels and efficiency (sensitivity) in experimenting to discern if there is any speaker distortion.

■ AUDIO ACCESSORIES

Other technological breakthroughs are also taking place in audio. Increased use of microprocessors provides sophisticated audio equipment with a high level of convenience and ease of use. Electronic tuning systems automatically fine-tune radio stations at the touch of a button, eliminating the endless rotation of the more traditional tuning knob; microprocessor memories permit listeners to preset favorite station frequencies for instant recall. Microprocessors can also enable listeners to program turntables and cassette decks to play specific selections on a tape or record in any sequence desired. Many turntables, tuners, amplifiers, receivers, and cassette decks can now be remotely controlled with microprocessing capabilities.

Optimizing a basic audio system can enhance listening pleasure. A number of add-on devices such as equalizers, noise reduction units, dynamic range expanders, and time delay systems are readily available. An **equalizer** allows the listener to shape the tonal quality of music and tailor the audio system to fit the sonic characteristics of the listening room. Graphic equalizers can substantially alter the quality of musical reproduction. They divide up the audible frequency spectrum into a number of separately controlled bands thereby evening out (equalizing) the frequency response of imperfect listening rooms and speakers. A "graphic" equalizer has its slide controls arranged like points on a graph showing just what frequency modifications the equalizer is contributing. Graphic equalizers are available from simple five-band stereo units to those that provide eight or ten controls per channel to cover the audible spectrum.

Noise-reduction units and **dynamic-range expanders** can correct flaws introduced into the music during the recording and broadcasting process. Due to the inability of present-day program sources (tape, disc, or FM radio) to capture the full dynamic range, a dynamic-range expander was developed. As the name suggests, it senses the instantaneous loudness levels of material passing through it and makes the loud moments of music louder and the quieter passages still softer in an attempt to restore the full dynamic range of music as it would sound at a live performance. Expanders usually have a control that adjusts the degree of expansion to suit the type of music being played.

Another device designed to enhance a system's sound is an audio **time-delay unit** or reverberation generator. This requires an additional pair of speakers and a second stereo amplifier, but when properly used it can create the feeling of the acoustical spaciousness of a concert hall within the smaller confines of a living room.

Another accessory is the **moving coil (MC) cartridge**, renowned for its brilliance and superb reproduction of musical 'transients,' the sharp attacks associated with cymbals, bells, triangles, and other percussive instruments. MC cartridges usually put out a smaller signal level than the more conventional types and so must generally be used with a step-up transformer or pre-amplifier, unless the additional circuitry is already contained in the amp or receiver.

Additional accessories called **optimizers** improve or expand the capabilities of an existing audio system. Turntable mats, disc stabilizers, and turntable insulators reduce spurious resonances during disc playback for clearer sound reproduction. There are gauges that help achieve proper stylus force, timers to turn audio equipment on and off at predetermined times, stands to elevate speakers for better dispersion and sound reproduction. The list goes on to include monitor/display units that "read out" operations of audio equipment, enabling users to make adjustments for better performance; switching and selector units that permit convenient interfacing of a variety of equipment in an audio component system; and cabinets for the attractive display or enclosure of audio components.

Also to be considered are record and tape care and equipment maintenance products. These encompass cleaners of all types, static neutralizers, demagnetizers, tape splicers, record sleeves, record and tape carrying cases and cabinets, and tape repair and editing kits.

Technical advice and consultation by Cliff Shumaker and Hal Pontez.

A useful video accessory is the PROC AMP by Vidicraft, a video processing amplifier designed to correct color and contrast errors.

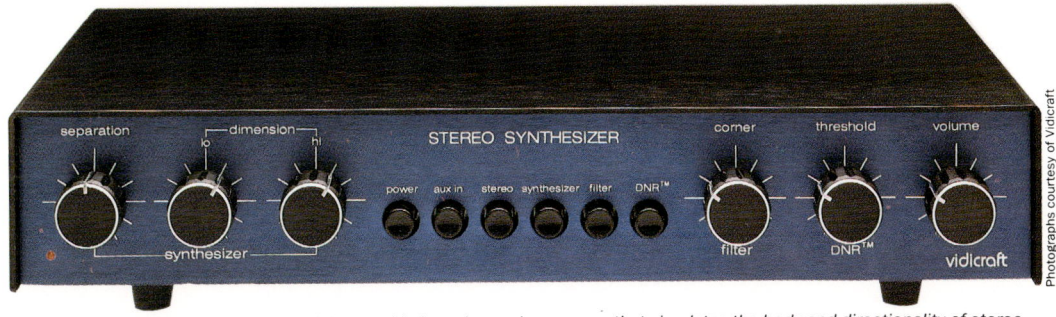
The STEREO SYNTHESIZER by Vidicraft is a sophisticated sound processor that simulates the body and directionality of stereo.

Project Designs

The technological climate of the 1980s has encouraged a new and sophisticated residential design outlook. While each era defines for itself a new standard of luxury, this one has settled on the home as its ideal. And with that commitment comes a strong desire to bring the world of electronic entertainment and communication to a very personal level. While this idea is as exciting to some people as it is abhorrent to others, for the designer and architect it translates into a new point of intersection between interior design and electronics.

No longer a pastiche of design clichés, electronic integration has reached a new level of sophistication. Advanced high-fidelity systems and large-screen projection televisions are now making their way into the home. Their look, however, is different. Sensitive product design is at least partially responsible. No longer objects of quaint affection, components are more discreet and simple than years ago. More importantly, however, is their mode of incorporation into the mainstream of a space. In a relatively short period of time, imaginative and elegant solutions have demonstrated a new sympathy between the electronic components and the space that contains them. With this comes a functional compatibility; a sitting room can now function as a film library, game room, screening room, and work station—all without compromising the integrity of the room's overall design.

PROJECT DESIGNS

◀ *More a statement of art than electronics, designer Adam Tihany discreetly showcased an entertainment system against a backdrop of restrained architectural minimalism.*

Photograph by Mark Ross

Elegant Restraint

Elegant restraint is the obvious keynote of this apartment designed by Adam Tihany. Furniture, art, and even accessories are few yet bold and luxurious. Shades of ivory in a variety of textures underscore the explicit minimalism, while a black ceiling heightens the drama. Seating was arranged along the perimeter walls to maintain the feeling of spaciousness without calling undue attention to the audio and video components. This is an acknowledgment of his client's paramount requirement—that such media equipment be incidental rather than critical to his enjoyment of the space. Both designer and client agreed, however, that its exclusion would be a mistake.

Tihany housed the components—Sony amplifier, preamplifier, tuner, equalizer and Zenith television—in a wall that he extended and curved around into an adjacent dining room. A separate ivory lacquer cabinet was then set flush within this nonstructural addition. Components are vertically stacked and bounded by narrow compartments for record storage and for the television cable box. The television is fixed at eye level and conveniently mounted on a pull-out drawer that also swivels. Proper ventilation is ensured by a pair of horizontal slits at the top of the cabinet.

MEDIA DESIGN

32

PROJECT DESIGNS

◀ An integrated audio-video system is the focal point of this library by Angelo Donghia. Components are flush-mounted in a custom, lacquer cabinet banded in brass.

Seating in the library is ▶ arranged for comfort and ease of viewing. A pair of bookcases flanks the sofa while a Francis Bacon triptych completes the vignette.

Townhouse Study

The library of this New York townhouse—designed by Angelo Donghia—is the setting for an integrated audio-video entertainment center. All of the components are flush-mounted in a custom-made lacquer cabinet accented with horizontal brass banding. Ample storage for records and tapes is provided behind pressure sensitive doors along the top and bottom of the unit. An Akai GK400D SS reel-to-reel tape deck is the fulcrum of the audio portion. It is flanked by Sansui's AU-2000 integrated amplifier and TU-7700 tuner and Technics' SL-1300 turntable (on the left) and by an Akai cassette deck and Ster-a-mote distribution system on the right. The Ster-a-mote permits full music control in the primary listening area as well as its disbursement to speakers located throughout the house. A pair of rosewood finished Celestion SL-6 compact monitors is discreetly hidden. The television is a 19-inch color set by Zenith. Audio-video system design is by Audio Command.

Photographs by Jaime Ardiles-Arce

MEDIA DESIGN

Simultaneous Recording

Conceived as an architectural palette, this apartment designed by Robert Bray and Michael Schaible of Bray-Schaible Design, Inc. perfectly orchestrates the art of design with the science of technology. A sophisticated audio system was an important part of the design effort throughout the residence. The owner's major requirement was that he be able to simultaneously record several broadcasts, each originating in a different city.

Components are flush-mounted in a custom matte, black cabinet located in a narrow pantry off the living area. The equipment profile includes several SAE FM tuners visible on the upper left side of the cabinet. A pair of Technics turntables, conveniently mounted on slide-out dollies, allows for mixing material on records with other sources. The primary recording decks are TEAC A-6600s. Four SAE amplifiers permit listeners to hear different programs in a number of areas throughout the apartment—and everything is controlled by a custom-designed switching system. Speakers were selected in accordance with the space and include B&W 801 monitors for the two main listening areas and ADS 300s in the smaller rooms. Audio System Design is by Dave Clark, The Sound Contact.

A custom-designed ▶ control panel beside the banquette permits full remote operation of the apartment's audio system. In addition to the remote switching devices there is an open well for a telephone and answering machine.

PROJECT DESIGNS

◀ In this apartment by Robert Bray and Michael Schaible, the primary audio components are flush-mounted in a custom cabinet adjacent to the living area. Four FM tuners permit simultaneous monitoring of several broadcasts.

Photographs by Jaime Ardiles-Arce

MEDIA DESIGN

Family Gatherings

A background of hand-carved paneling enhances this contemporary library/media room designed by Noel Jeffrey. With seating, dining, and entertainment needs amply met, the room encourages the informal gatherings for which it was intended.

Jeffrey's first order of business was to update the dark, paneled walls. A laborious process of scraping, bleaching, and glazing effectively restored the room's vitality. As the owners had clearly outlined their needs—a comfortable room for small suppers, watching television, reading, and listening to music—Jeffrey finished the space with characteristic style. A custom designed L-shaped banquette—the curves of which echo a subtle Art Deco flair—was specified for a corner. An upholstered chair and ottoman and a custom coffee table complete that end of the room. Situated by the window, a set of leather and tubular steel chairs surround a granite-topped dining table.

The media cabinet is another custom design by Jeffrey. Fabricated in bird's-eye maple, it features a lighted niche and pivoting television tray for the 25-inch Sony Profeel. A videocassette recorder by JVC is stored behind the cabinet's lower doors.

With respect for their outstanding design, it was decided that the Bang & Olufsen audio components (Beomaster 2400 and Beocord 5000) should remain in full view inside the bookcase.

PROJECT DESIGNS

◀ *The media/storage cabinet is fabricated in bird's-eye maple and features a lighted interior niche and pivoting television tray. The unit is crowned with a sculpture by Louise Nevelson.*

The softly curved ▶ banquette is sympathetic with the arched cornice above the recessed bookshelves. Bang & Olufsen components are located on the bottom shelf for easiest access.

Photographs by Derrick and Love

MEDIA DESIGN

A Sense of Drama

A sense of the dramatic figures prominently in all of Sam Lopata's work. In consistently avoiding the austerity ethic he uses contrasting materials and theatrical lighting to evoke a heightened architectural awareness.

Simple yet effective architectural devices are the cornerstone of Lopata's plan for this apartment. A rather large column was used to create spatial definition between the living room and foyer. An application of black slate tiles on the floor and column further silhouettes this definition with added graphic impact.

Lighting is used for drama and theatrical effect. A series of dropped coves and ceiling niches was created to house bands of pink and blue neon. Providing the architectural *tour de force*, a simple cutout allows the column to visually "indent" the ceiling for the illusion of greater height and diminished stature.

Fine contemporary art and black leather seating from Pace qualify the white-walled living room. The media equipment is ingeniously housed in a black laminate cabinet set into the face of the column. Special features include a full-width drawer to accommodate side-by-side turntables plus open shelves below for record album storage with room to expand.

◀ Artfully placed inside the column, the media system becomes one with the architecture. Ceiling coves and niches accommodate bands of pink and blue neon. Painting by Lesley Dill is Woman in a Shower.

▲ Black slate tiles silhouette the foyer with dramatic impact. Media equipment is housed in the column at right, facing the living room. Painting is by Dubuffet.

Photographs by Derrick and Love

MEDIA DESIGN

A Comfortable Retreat

Superbly elegant yet always inviting—as is all of Katherine Stephens's work—this room was conceived as a personal retreat for a busy professional couple. Ultimate comfort is assured with such amenities as a bathroom-turned-bar, two telephones, and a pair of chaise lounges covered in silver gray moiré. In consideration of the couple's differing taste in television programming, Stephens designed this unique video entertainment center. Three 12-inch televisions are flush-mounted in a matte black cabinet atop a polished steel frame. Three pictures can be simultaneously tuned with the sound controlled by a wireless remote. The use of individual headsets allows for maximum flexibility. In addition to the video, an antique walnut backgammon table and writing desk complete the room's appointments. Coloration is intentionally subdued. Complementing the mauve/gray walls, a pink ceiling enhances the natural quality of light in the room. Investment art—Lilla Cabot Perry's *The Yellow Rose* flanked by two Mary Cassatt drawings—are romantically suspended from grosgrain ribbons.

PROJECT DESIGNS

◀ An antique backgammon table and writing table make the room conducive to the pursuit of leisurely activities. Formal window treatment adds a note of period grace.

Katherine Stephens's ▶ custom-designed video entertainment unit consists of three 12-inch Sony televisions flush-mounted in a matte black cabinet. Individual headsets and wireless remote control permits maximum flexibility.

Photographs by Bill Rothschild

MEDIA DESIGN

▶ White oak tables in the dining area and living room counterpoint this sleek, all-white environment. A centralized audio system is contained behind panels of the mirrored living room wall. The white coffee table with sliding trays is a custom design by Montoya.

◀ Two mirrored panels on the living room wall open onto a complete audio system. The equipment is shelf-mounted inside a cabinet covered with brushed strainless steel.

Photographs by Norman McGrath

Ocean Penthouse

Juan Montoya is articulate in his work: Themes are laid down with unmistakable clarity. In this Florida penthouse, the designer has created an interior that is both urbane and dramatic—a considerable accomplishment considering the strictures of an all-white color palette.

Montoya has directed the ingredients of this interior with careful thought and restraint. White ceramic floor tiles set the stage with a feeling of cool spaciousness. Furnishings were kept to a minimum to enhance the feeling of openness. White modular seating units are complemented by a pair of classic Breuer armchairs with tubular steel frames. Coffee tables include a white oak drum table and a plastic laminate cube with slide-out trays designed by Montoya.

Recessed nautical lights define the raised dining platform, appointed with a custom dining table and Knoll chairs. Mirror was generously used along a living room wall to amplify the space and reflect the ocean view. This same wall features two floor-to-ceiling mirror panels that conceal a former closet turned media cabinet. Audio components are stacked inside on a cabinet sheathed in brushed stainless steel. Since the entire apartment was wired for sound, there are speakers in every room of the penthouse. Audio installation is by Lyric Hi-Fi.

PROJECT DESIGNS

▲ Resembling the base of a truncated pyramid, the television cabinet is mounted on the mirrored wall opposite the bed.

◀ Raising the bed on a carpeted platform gave the owners easier access to the view. Speakers are flush-mounted in the wall-mounted cabinets, designed as counterparts to the triangular bedside tables.

Photographs by Norman McGrath

MEDIA DESIGN

Library Entertainment

Conceived in the tradition of its seventeenth-century birthright, this multi-purpose library—designed by Robert Metzger—clearly demonstrates the sympathetic commingling of tradition and technology. With his eye for historical quotation Metzger has preserved the room's natural character while fully meeting the demands of modern living and state-of-the-art entertaining.

With architectural assets seldom encountered in today's spaces, Metzger restored the original coffered ceiling, stone hearth, and paneled walls. Against this implicit background a mélange of fine antiques and richly upholstered furnishings imbue the space with unexpected warmth and personality. Though outwardly a library, the room enjoys a far more profound identity. Replete with dining alcove, seating area, and work space, it adequately serves a full range of needs—from business to social.

Never one to ignore the current technology, Metzger collaborated with Art Powers-Designed Sound on an entertainment system. In this case Powers planned the system, chose the components, and installed them—all while maintaining the integrity of Metzger's design.

The shelves were removed from an antique bookcase—one of a pair flanking the stone chimneypiece—to accommodate the new equipment. A lacquered cabinet with smoked glass doors was designed by Metzger to fit inside the now-open bookcase (Powers approved the specifications along the way).

A profile of the audio equipment selected includes a Teac reel-to-reel tape player, Mitsubishi vertical turntable, Sony digital tuner, Teac cassette deck, Designed Sound amplifier (custom), and dbx noise reduction unit. Sixteen ADS speakers complete the total surround system. A Digital switching system can access five separate sound sources into five different rooms via a sixteen-button control panel. The video profile includes two RCA 25-inch monitors, a Pioneer Video Laserdisc player, and a Commodore 64 computer set up to display on one of the monitors.

A pair of 25-inch color video monitors are the focal point of the entertainment system. The components are housed in a three-part custom-designed lacquer cabinet with smoked glass doors.

PROJECT DESIGNS

The banquette-lined dining alcove is well suited for intimate suppers or small business conferences. The lacquer table is from Ron Seff.

Recalling the grandeur of a bygone era, this Fifth Avenue library was designed to meet the demands of modern living and entertaining. The room features outstanding architectural detail, fine antiques, and a state-of-the-art entertainment system. ▼

Photographs by Jaime Ardiles-Arce

MEDIA | DESIGN

▲ A soaring two story window frames a spectacular view of the New York skyline. The lacquer frame sofa, custom designed by Kuhn, features three outdoor steplights recessed along each side; reading lamps are built in.

Atelier in Gray

Dazzling by night and just as dramatic by day, this spacious New York apartment was designed by Gerald Kuhn. Managing the two-story space, however, required an experienced sense of scale. Kuhn used luxurious furnishings with clean, simple lines and a soothing gray color palette to successfully address the issue. Collectively, his approach manages a strength sufficient enough to match the grandiose scale of the room.

The main living room is a shrewd mixture of expansiveness and intimacy. The sides of the room that overlook Central Park feature 20-foot windows, while the adjoining "balconied" wall carries a much lower elevation. Credit for this quality rests squarely on Kuhn. Using simple architectural devices Kuhn enlarged the balcony by flattening its original trapezoidal shape; he added new fissures (now qualified with pipe railing) to lighten the once-enclosed area.

Furnishings are arranged to create internal zones, one facing the Park, the other toward the fireplace. The catalyst of the arrangement is a large two-sided sofa. Designed by Kuhn especially for this space, it features a gray lacquer frame that incorporates the backrest, side tables, and reading lamps. Suede-covered tub chairs and polished steel-drum tables complement the setting.

Kuhn created a unique sculpted media/storage cabinet at the foot of the stairs. A model of design ingenuity, its profile is stepped in a series of progressive elevations. Fabricated in a combination of materials—laminate for the horizontal surfaces and lacquer for the vertical ones—the cabinet's practicality is further underscored by its modular construction (there are six separate pieces).

Storage was well-planned to anticipate the needs of a burgeoning album and tape collection; eight cupboard doors, eighteen drawers, and ten cassette trays accommodate audio storage needs, while six large doors along the bottom conceal speakers and video components.

A lift-up lid opens to reveal the audio components, all vertically flush-mounted as a space-saving measure. The equipment profile includes a Bang & Olufsen Beogram 8000, McIntosh MAC 4100 receiver, and a Dual C839RC auto-reverse cassette deck. One speaker was placed in the bottom of the cabinet behind a cutout door; the other speaker was subtly flush-mounted in the balcony overhang. Both the Zenith 25-inch System III Space Command color television and RCA Selectavision videocassette recorder are mounted on slide-out dollies in the cabinet.

▲ The stepped profile of the media/storage cabinet is a substantial architectural statement. A cutout door on the lower right reveals one of the speakers; another speaker is flush-mounted in the balcony. The painting on the back wall is by Graham Dean; over the fireplace, a Frank Stella.

Photographs by Derrick and Love

◄ Variable size drawers were planned for the storage of record albums and tapes. The lift-up lid reveals a selection of vertically flush-mounted audio components; the videocassette recorder sits on a sliding dolly.

DESIGN

Paneled Concealment

Clean, simple lines and comfortable furnishings distinguish this apartment designed by Barbara Ross, ASID, and Barbara Schwartz, ASID, of Dexter Design Inc. Most outstanding, however, is the network of custom built-ins that runs throughout the entire apartment. Etagères, bookcases, and wall niches have been orchestrated to increase storage capacity while, at the same time, adding architectural clarity to the space.

An audio-video system is the focal point of the living room. Maintaining the apartment's understated look, the entire system was flush-mounted behind floor-to-ceiling ash panels. As one of several discrete systems in the apartment, it offers a full range of entertainment possibilities. Seating is arranged to allow for a comfortably unobstructed view of the television monitor. An L-shaped banquette was placed on an angle along with a pair of tub chairs mounted on pivoting bases. Recessed floodlights are set into the newly constructed ceiling soffits along the room's perimeter.

Cliff Shumaker and Hal Pontez, The Audio Consultant, designed and installed the system with quality and performance in mind. Since the clients wanted maximum flexibility and user independence, a total of four systems were installed throughout the apartment. In the living room components were selected in accordance with the clients' sonic expectations.

Sony's Audio Lab components were selected (TK88 tuner, preamplifier, and cassette deck) along with a McIntosh amplifier 2155. A Mitsubishi Linear Tracking Turntable is hidden from sight inside its own drawer beneath the monitor. Sound is driven through four high-quality B&W mini-monitors. They are scattered about the living room: One is shelf-mounted in the tall bookcase next to the doorway; another is shelf-mounted in the low bookcase behind the sofa; the remaining two are flush-mounted in the opposite wall behind fabric grilles. This same system also feeds the dining room through a pair of Pyramid 7 speakers. The living room video components include a Sony KX2501 25-inch high resolution color monitor (on a slide-out tray), a Sony VTX1000R tuner and a JVC HR765OU VHS unit.

Dexter Design's efficient storage plan continues into the master bedroom. Closets, a dressing table, and even a window seat were all built-in for maximum space utilization. Floor-to-ceiling panels—this time executed in beige laminate—are once again used to conceal the audio-video system. For this room Shumaker and Pontez chose components in light of spatial as well as aesthetic considerations. On the audio side, an AIWA 808 micro system was selected. Sound is driven through a pair of Canton GL260s, flush-mounted beneath the window seat. For video there is a Sony KV1945 RS 19-inch receiver/monitor and a JVC HL765OU videocassette recorder. As an added convenience the entire system is operable from the bed.

▲ A series of floor-to-ceiling ash panels conceals ample storage space and a fully integrated audio-video system. The antique gramophone is from the owner's extensive collection; on the back wall, Ariste Bruant by Toulouse Lautrec.

Simple by design and ▶ easy to operate, the entertainment system is the focal point of the living room. Special convenience features include a turntable drawer and video monitor pivoting tray. On the wall, La revue blanche by Toulouse Lautrec.

PROJECT DESIGNS

◂ *A separate audio-video system is built into a wall of storage in the master bedroom. Mirror panels dramatize the window-seat view of Manhattan.*

Photographs by Derrick and Love

MEDIA | DESIGN

Le Grand Salon

Few challenges could hold such demands as producing a contemporary statement within a space of awesome traditional character. Such was the case in this grande salon created by Michael de Santis. Directoire paneling (already painted and gilded), marble chimneypiece, and papered ceiling were all original features that could not be altered in any way. De Santis's solution was to subtly reiterate—and in some instances, counterpoint—the room's formality with a mixture of contemporary furnishings, art, and accessories.

Taking its cue from the panel color, upholstered seating is covered in moss-green perforated suede. The entire grouping is asymmetrically placed and anchored by a marble-topped table from Les Prismatiques. Brass is generously used throughout the room—lamps, console tables, window frames and even sofa plinths—as an elegant accent.

A sophisticated audio system completes this opulent setting. A custom-made cabinet from Pace—black lacquer with smoked glass doors and brass trim—houses a full complement of matte black components. Designed and installed by Audio Command the system includes Audio Command terminal model #6, Audio Command power supply, ACS panel model #8002, SAE A-201 power amplifier, SAE P-101 preamplifier, SAE E-101 equalizer, SAE T-101 digital tuner, Sansui D770RB auto-reverse cassette deck, Bang & Olufsen #8002 turntable and cartridge, TEAC X10000RB auto-reverse reel-to-reel, and Canton 510 speakers.

◀ Contemporary furnishings, art, and accessories underscore the opulence of this traditional paneled salon. Stage-inspired lighting forms an open canopy above the main seating area.

For ease of access, ▶ matte black audio components were flush-mounted on an angle inside a brass-trimmed cabinet from Pace. A wide brass border outlines the perimeter of the floor, while narrower brass bands traverse the space in a diagonal pattern.

PROJECT DESIGNS

Photographs by Jaime Ardiles-Arce

DESIGN

Fantasy Sequence

Designer Mario Lo Cicero has demonstrated uninhibited originality in this studio apartment/screening room. Preferring the freedom of an experimental palette, the designer creates unique visual imagery with theatrical sleight-of-hand. Here the designer's jangled images mix with a variety of design cues for a lesson in very personal style.

Like most studio apartments, this one—although comfortably proportioned—lacked the essence of "fugitive domain." Lo Cicero resolved the issue by designing a loft bed which effectively created an alcove office, sleeping aerie, and as an added bonus, plenty of storage space.

A fabric-draped wall treatment is the decorative mainstay of the apartment's transformation; walls are loosely swagged with yards and yards of white parachute silk for a look that closely resembles a Hollywood dream sequence. On the ceiling, fabric was fastened along the edge of the room and gathered around a Mirrex disc for a canopied effect. The generous use of mirror on the loft bed, mantle, and chimney adds sparkle and multiple images.

A variety of design cues encompass the playful and the classic: white rubber flooring overlaid with a polished steel grid is almost glamorous under the gaze of a rotating mirror ball. A pair of molded fiberglass 'Gyro' chairs designed by Eero Aarnio solicit a juvenile response, especially in the company of colorfully gelled fluorescents.

Yet for all its fantasy, the room enjoys a double identity; at the touch of a button a projection screen is lowered from its ceiling recess in front of the fireplace. The projector is neatly concealed in a niche cut into the side of the loft bed; this also permits the alcove office (equipped with a complete Sony audio system) to function as the projection room.

◀ Parachute silk draped on the walls and ceiling creates a fantasy atmosphere in this studio apartment. Mirrored panels, gelled fluorescent lights, and a white rubber floor treatment heighten the imagery.

◀ The alcove office beneath the loft bed is equipped with a desk, book and storage shelves, as well as a complete audio system; it also functions as the projection room during a screening.

To set the room for an ▶ evening's film, a projection screen is electronically lowered from its ceiling enclosure. The projector is housed across the room in the side of the loft bed.

Photographs by Jaime Ardiles-Arce

MEDIA DESIGN

Entertainment Tower

A free-standing media column and new wet bar have instilled this sitting room with unforseen entertainment potential. Designed by Barbara Ross, ASID, and Barbara Schwartz, ASID, of Dexter Design Inc., the once seldom-used room has now become the clients' favorite.

Located immediately off the foyer of a spacious duplex, the room featured a needless entry into the dining room, a full bath, and an undistinguished view. The clients wanted to enliven the space with a design statement of sufficient identity to enhance rather than overwhelm their collection of fine contemporary art.

Considerable structural efforts were expended to attain the final outcome. The dining room access was sealed off and the bath became a powder room, its bathtub replaced by a wet bar, refrigerator, and ice maker. The gray lacquer media column was designed for convenience and practicality. Both the turntable and video monitor are mounted on slide-out trays (the monitor also pivots), while a hinged rear panel permits easy access for maintenance. At the top of the column on the equipment side is another hinged panel, which conceals the speaker selector box and cable television box.

Cliff Shumaker and Hal Pontez, The Audio Consultant, designed and installed a system that integrates a full range of audio and video capabilities while maintaining an understated appearance. Flexibility and ease of operation are the keynotes. Audio, for example, can be exclusively heard in three rooms or in conjunction with video in one room and audio in the remaining two. The Audio Consultant further managed to incorporate a variety of source components within the limiting confines of a vertical tower. Effective component selection was critical to the solution. Consider the use of the Bang & Olufsen Beogram 1800—capable of being started *after* the record is in place and the slide tray has been returned to its original position; it eliminated the need for an oversize turntable compartment. A front-loading VCR was also selected for its space saving features. The Audio Consultant assembled the following equipment profile: Yamaha Natural Sound stereo receiver R-100, Nakamichi LX-3 two head cassette deck, Bang & Olufsen Beogram 1800 turntable, NEC 25-inch Auto Color video monitor, JVC HR76500 videocassette recorder, NEC PLL television tuner/timer TU-831EN. Two Sony speakers are mounted on either side of the audio components just above the video monitor; a Sony digital disc player CDP101, purchased after the cabinet was installed, is shelf-mounted in a hidden cabinet adjacent to the bar.

▶ A gray lacquer media column lends architectural significance to this all-gray sitting room. The top panel conceals additional storage space as well as the television cable and speaker selector boxes. The painting is by Alex Katz.

Photograph by Derrick and Love

MEDIA DESIGN

Separating the public and private areas of this apartment, a large black cabinet incorporates a pair of flush-mounted speakers on either end.

Sound Design

Glossy white walls and all-black furnishings make a classic design statement in this apartment by Bray-Schaible Design, Inc. In keeping with the client's wishes the project called for a simple interior with ample seating space and a discreetly placed audio system. The first need was satisfied with large custom banquettes and a carpeted platform running nearly the full length of the window wall. A black monolithic cabinet separating the public and private areas of the apartment solved the audio problem with architectural practicality. As housing for the loudspeakers—and to give them a built-in look—grille cloths were removed and holes were cut in the cabinet to reveal only the woofers, midrange, and tweeter domes while concealing the rest of the speaker itself. The opposite side of the cabinet was left open to reveal ample shelf storage as well as space for the audio components. An additional pair of ADS 801 speakers were shelf-mounted to direct music into the bedroom portion of the apartment.

The back of the cabinet was left open for easy access to the audio components and library. An additional set of ADS 801 speakers are shelf-mounted in the uppermost right and left compartments, which permits unobstructed music to be heard in the apartment's private sector.

The black speaker cabinet and structural column reiterate the boundary of the apartment's public and private areas. For maximum flexibility, adjustable light fixtures are clamped onto a polished steel rod and plugged into a junction box at the base of the column.

Photographs by Jaime Ardiles-Arce

MEDIA DESIGN

Architectural Enclaves

In an apartment designed by Bob Patino and Vincent Wolf, functional compatibility is suggested rather than clearly defined. Columns, partitions, and surface treatments effectively create a series of enclaves that invite activity and instill structural harmony.

Removing the apartment's existing walls liberated the space and incorporated a panoramic skyline view. Champagne-colored walls, Travertine marble floor treatment, and luxurious furnishings are the makings of this sophisticated urban retreat high above the city.

The open-plan study is a microcosm of the design principles evident throughout the apartment; a large architectural column intimates its existence, while a carpeted floor treatment more clearly defines its perimeter. Custom-designed furnishings include the suede banquette and white oak table with telescoping pedestal base. A pair of steel-framed and leather Brno chairs completes the vignette.

A white oak cabinet is recessed into a column, reiterating the harmony between decoration and architecture. The cabinet is intelligently planned to articulate function and beauty. Equipment is flush-mounted at a height calculated for ease of operation; tape storage drawers and a slide-out tray for the VCR are featured.

As the central audio system for the apartment's public space, components include a tuner, amplifier, and cassette deck from Hitachi. Sony speakers are flush-mounted in the adjacent wall and throughout the entire apartment. A Sony 19-inch color televison and videocassette recorder complete the video profile.

Components are flush-mounted in a white oak cabinet custom-designed by Patino/Wolf; tape storage drawers and a slide-out tray for the VCR are featured details. A telescoping pedestal base—also a custom design—adjusts the table to any desired height.

◀Architectural fissures were orchestrated to create enclaves of activity and frame skyline views. An imposing column, with an integrated media cabinet, spatially defines the study; the carpet is antique Persian.

Photographs by Peter Vitale

PROJECT DESIGNS

MEDIA DESIGN

▲ White vinyl panels with brass strips highlight one of the apartment's main structural columns. Black and white pony skin rugs add graphic impact against the otherwise all white background.

In a wall of brushed ▶ aluminum cabinetry, Montoya enclosed a large television screen with a radius-cornered niche. The white glass and lacquer coffee table was custom-designed with a stepped profile to house the television projector. Storage space on either side of the screen (concealed by doors) contains a built-in bar and audio system.

PROJECT DESIGNS

Screening Niche

Juan Montoya's design for this New York penthouse is sleekly opulent. With an intentionally limited palette, brass, lacquer, and terrazzo surface treatments mingle throughout the 7,000-square-foot apartment to qualify the space with mood and visual texture.

Involved with the project since the outset of the building's construction, Montoya planned gracious public rooms for large-scale entertaining. Although the plan called for a flow of space, each room was planned with a separate yet compatible identity. Montoya cleverly used brass accents to enhance the room's fluidity and overall pervasiveness: Brass friezes and floorboards interconnect throughout the entire space, while the terrazzo flooring was overlaid with a brass windowpane grid; vertical brass strips highlight the new architectural columns in the living room as well.

The den/media room varies these cues for a change in mood—white terrazzo flooring and brass trim are replaced with carpeting and brushed aluminum for a softer more restrained look.

The design of the room was substantially determined by a large-screen projection television (Kloss). Separating the den and the living room is a wall of brushed aluminum cabinetry of the simplest design. At the focus of the cabinet, a large niche with radius corners—its interior painted black for greater picture contrast—accepts the 5-foot television screen. Full-height door panels flanking the screen can be opened for access to a built-in bar, Rotel stereo system, and general storage. The projector is artfully concealed in the coffee table, custom-designed by Montoya. Fabricated in white glass and lacquer, its stepped profile accommodates the light path of the triple lens unit. Seating was arranged with deference to the room's major attraction.

Photographs by Jaime Ardiles-Arce

MEDIA | DESIGN

▲ A switch panel designed by Lawrence provides additional audio conveniences. Speaker control for the second level of the apartment can be regulated in the sitting room, office, master bedroom, and gymnasium.

Songwriter's Perfection

Designer Jack Debman Lawrence has created a private world of quiet splendor in this New York duplex. Beneath a façade of fine antiques and artwork, however, lies a flawlessly purring machine that was conceived to enhance the musical pleasure of his songwriter client. What makes this apartment so special is Lawrence's unyielding eye for perfection; he accommodates even the most incidental details with great style and judgment.

Acknowledging his client's personal and professional regard for music, Lawrence (together with audio consultant Holly Neil) provided audio throughout the residence with two centralized systems. The first is located in the upper-level picture gallery and serves both floors of the apartment; a

Photographs by Derrick and Love

PROJECT DESIGNS

◀ The upstairs audio system is flush-mounted in a custom-designed ash cabinet at the head of the picture gallery. Just beneath the lighted recess, panels open to reveal the system's wiring, all of which is color-coded for ease of maintenance. Mounted over each of the open-reel tape decks is a pair of small monitor speakers.

The kitchen audio ▶ system is mounted in a wall of ash cabinetry. A Technics Linear Tracking turntable is raised on an angle for easier operation. The cabinet's interior recesses are automatically illuminated when the cabinet doors are opened.

MEDIA DESIGN

◀ Setting a classic vignette, French armchairs in the Empire style flank a Japanese lacquer table. Carrado Cagli's King Solomon hangs over the white marble chimneypiece. Mounted on plywood backing, the painting swings open like a door to reveal a television (below left). Hung on the back of the "door" is Picasso's Venus et l'Amour. An eighteenth-century Flemish armoire at right is fitted with a built-in bar; glazed Japanese roof tiles are displayed on top.

Neo-Georgian paneling ▶ sets a casual note in the songwriter's office. Amid a collection of personal mementos an audio system is flush-mounted in the space beneath the bookcase; speakers are contained in the radiator enclosures beneath each window. The eighteenth-century English rosewood desk features a slant-top enclosure and tooled leather writing surface.

PROJECT DESIGNS

Photographs by Derrick and Love

second system, located in the kitchen, drives sound throughout the first floor exclusively.

The second-floor audio system is located in a former closet adjacent to a picture gallery. From this position, music can be accurately controlled throughout the entire apartment. For storage and display Lawrence designed an ash cabinet with every conceivable convenience in mind. The two-part cabinet was designed around a central, lighted recess. The upper portion contains two open-reel tape decks (Akai GX635D and a Teac 3300) along with a pair of mini minotor speakers for accurate volume and tone control. The mirrored recess accommodates a turntable, ample space for record albums, and a bronze-finished control panel. Designed by Lawrence, its nine toggle switches regulate speaker control throughout the second floor and expedite dubbing and duplicating in four directions on either tape format. The rest of the audio components are flush-mounted in the enclosure below. Attending to every detail, Lawrence designed narrow panels beneath the recess which open to reveal the system's wiring, all of which is color-coded and labeled for ease of maintenance. The equipment includes an Akai stereo cassette deck GXF90; ADC stereo frequency equalizer (Sound Shaper Two MkII), Onkyo quartz-locked stereo receiver TX8500MkII, and an Akai quick-reverse stereo cassette deck GXC-735D. There are also two cassette tape storage drawers. The entire cabinet—with the exception of the middle recess—can be concealed behind sets of bi-fold doors.

The sitting room across from the picture gallery shows Lawrence's fine hand in orchestrating a refined selection of art and antiques. Although the room was planned for intimate evenings outside the formal living room, the mood is nonetheless considerably elegant. An eighteenth-century English chimneypiece in white marble is the room's architectural highlight. Using it as an unexpected "stage," Lawrence placed an antique Japanese terra-cotta tomb figure inside the fireplace instead of

MEDIA | DESIGN

◀ A pair of eighteenth-century Japanese screens are wall-mounted above the bed. Depicting the Tokugawa Shogunate, their gold-leaf finish enhances the quality of light throughout the room.

▲ A full-function control panel is located in an extension drawer beside the bed. The alarm system with code and panic buttons is located here as well as the electric blanket control, digital clock, and five-line telephone with intercom. There is also a master switch to control lighting throughout the entire apartment and in the room; a special tissue compartment and storage bin is also included.

the usual andirons. Setting a classic vignette, French armchairs in the Biedermeir style are poised on either side of a small Japanese lacquer table. Over the chimneypiece, Carrado Cagli's *King Solomon* is the mainstay of Lawrence's inspired sleight-of-hand. Mounted on a one-quarter-inch plywood backing, the painting swings open like a door to reveal a television mounted in the unused flue. For a final touch of the unexpected, Lawrence hung the back of the "door" with another etching—Picasso's *Venus et l'Amour*. To visually finish the enclosure, the television (Sony 19-inch KV2142R Trinitron with wireless remote control) features a custom-designed brass plinth incorporating a digital clock and cable channel selector.

For the office, neo-Georgian paneling, dismantled from an English country house, sets a more casual tone than the sitting room. A collection of African artifacts, a piano, and a selection of theatrical posters publicizing the songwriter's Broadway productions add a more personal touch to this private domain. A very fine eighteenth-century English rosewood writing desk with slant top and leather-covered tub chair lend a certain elegance to the room. Lawrence provided a special audio system for the client's exclusive use. Flush-mounted beneath the book-lined niche, the cassette deck and tuner (and the microphone standing by the piano) permit the option of arranging as well as interfacing with the main system. Speakers in this room are also concealed in the radiator enclosures beneath the windows.

A pair of eighteenth-century Japanese screens depicting the Tokugawa Shogunate adds considerable aura to the master bedroom. A custom-designed white bleached-oak cabinet functions as headboard and storage facility. True to form, Lawrence has attended to every conceivable need. Extension drawers on either side of the bed feature brushed-brass control panels. Between the two panels there is total control of the second-floor audio system, the television, lighting throughout the apartment, and the burglar alarm. Recessed digital clocks, two telephones, and an intercom are also incorporated. Rather than opting for an overpowering video presence, Lawrence chose the flexibility of a Sony 9-inch KV-8000. A custom caddy on recessed casters allows for mobility around the entire bed for a more personal

PROJECT DESIGNS

The extension drawer to the right of the bed contains a brushed-brass control panel designed by Lawrence. A series of toggle switches controls the cable television box and channel selector, electric blanket, and room lights. A 9-inch Sony television sits inside a custom caddy mounted on casters for maximum flexibility.

viewing experience; telescoping cables neatly expedite this system. Speakers are flush-mounted in the window coves beside the bed.

With the first floor kitchen system, Lawrence sacrificed neither aesthetics nor sonics. Floor-to-ceiling ash panels discreetly conceal the sound center. Hinge-mounted light switches automatically illuminate the media wall upon opening the doors (one lighting recess is located at the top of the cabinet; the other is just above the turntable and record bin). The equipment is both flush-mounted and shelf-mounted with every conceivable storage need provided for. On the uppermost shelf flanked by a pair of covered crystal jars is a BIC Beam Box Model FM 10 Directable FM Antenna. Immediately below is a flush-mounted control panel designed by Lawrence. Finished in matte bronze, it features two power toggle switches on the left and four individual room switches on the right—two for the kitchen, one for the dining room, and one for the living room. The control panel permits music to be heard in any combination of the three rooms desired. A Sansui 5900Z Digital Synthesizer DC stereo receiver completes one portion of the profile.

An open compartment on the next level accommodates a Technics quartz direct-drive automatic SL15 linear tracking turntable. Lawrence placed it at a 45-degree angle for easy access. Immediately to the right is an album storage bin with a smaller utility drawer just beneath it. Flush-mounted under the turntable is an Akai quick-reverse stereo cassette deck 6XC-735D. A full-width tape storage drawer features custom compartments and an interior writing tray for notations when taping. General storage is concealed behind a pair of flush doors at the bottom of the cabinet.

A vertical column visually delineates the dining area from the food preparation area. It also functions as a housing for the 15-inch Sony EconoQuick KV1514 color television. A unique feature permits the column to be rotated a full 360 degrees to allow uninterrupted viewing from any corner of the kitchen. A bronze control panel also designed by Lawrence is flush-mounted above the television. It incorporates the cable tuner, digital clock, and power switches all together. Rheostat-controlled incandescent lighting gently filters through an antidazzling grille just above the dining top.

MEDIA | DESIGN

Baroque Electronics

The most arresting interior spaces are those that reverberate with the design cues of two distinct eras; skillful juxtaposition is crucial to a successful interior of this kind. In this executive's home computer room designed by Stanley Jay Friedman and associates Joel C. Gevis and Roger Urmson, Italian Baroque and high technology counterpoint in an idiom best described as "classical modernism."

With characteristic Friedman style, variations of a monochromatic palette—in this case, a slate green coloration—allows art, accessories, and even people to play a more exciting role in the completion of the space itself. In plan, the room is a rectangle with furnishings concentrated at the far end by the windows. Here, a custom leather banquette, table, and chairs (also executed in leather and designed by Friedman for Bonaventure) can accommodate a business conference, an intimate supper, or an evening of solitary relaxation. Classical references soften the otherwise severe approach—gilded putti and billowing Roman shades become the antithesis of twentieth-century electronic technology. With an eye toward the humorous, anatomical wall sconces—made from gilded mannequin arms—playfully recall Giacometti's classic design.

Although state-of-the-art electronics are an integral part of the space, Friedman and associates (together with Audio Command) designed the system to be discreet rather than assaulting. Flush-mounting along the side wall in a vertical configuration intelligently makes the components less focal, not less important.

Photographs by Peter Vitale

PROJECT DESIGNS

The flush-mounted media unit features an Audio Command control panel with telephone elevated on an angle and set into a lighted niche. A computer keyboard is directly connected to the color video monitor and illuminated with a flexible cueing light; a mirrored panel multiplies the imagery ad infinitum.

◀Leather-covered table and chairs designed by Stanley Jay Friedman are grouped around the discreetly placed media column. Italian Baroque gilded putti and Roman shades underscore the room's "classical modernism." Alphonse Osbert's L'Enigme (courtesy Barry Freidman, Ltd.) backs a crystal-laden console table in the foreground.

MEDIA DESIGN

Simplicity Defined

Cutout partitions and sweeping enclosures clarify spatial volumes in this apartment by Robert Bray and Michael Schaible. Walls were removed to liberate a series of enclosed anterooms and hallways; in somewhat of an irreverent gesture the original crown moldings were left in commemoration of their prior existence.

The interior's impact depends upon an inseparable melding of custom components, furnishings, and artwork. Consider the deep window recesses and lower wall, angled and trimmed with a picture ledge. Mingling with these cues is a seating enclave framed by a low retaining partition.

A state-of-the-art audio system was a major part of the design effort. A central system designed by Dave Clark, The Sound Contact, is housed in a wall niche at the foot of the stairs. Matte black components are flush-mounted in a black laminate cabinet, while a pair of turntables are fitted onto pull-out trays. The equipment includes Nakamichi 1000 cassette deck, Mark Levinson LNC2 crossover, Technics SP10 Mark II with Fidelity Research Arm and Koitsu cartridge, Technics SP600 record changer, two Mark Levinson amplifiers, Model I Sequerra FM tuner, Mark Levinson LMP5 premaplifier, B7K oscilloscope, Sound Concepts Digital Delay, SAE integrated amplifier. A pair of computer-grade fans are thermostatically controlled and cool the system automatically. Speakers throughout this level of the apartment include four Magneplanar woofers, two Magneplanar tweeters, two Allison I speakers, and assorted JBL tweeters.

▲ *A curved and polished steel partition protects a seating enclave from view. Closet and storage space is provided opposite.*

▶ *Speakers are built into the panels of a folding screen in the back of the living room. The wall beneath the windows was specially angled to display this series of engravings.*

Photographs by Jaime Ardiles-Arce

◄ The audio system of this apartment is housed in a wall niche at the foot of the stairs. A classic column strikes a note of architectural grandeur.

MEDIA DESIGN

Executive Suite

Created by Gensler and Associates, this office projects an informal character that more closely resembles a living room than a work space. Reflecting his personal taste and management style, the client is a New York based film producer whose primary office activities necessitate the viewing of videotapes and listening to sound tracks. The client requested that the system be visible from his desk as well as from a small conference table.

The space itself is small yet well planned and luxurious. A figured, black laminate storage wall clearly defines the fine furnishings and flush-mounted audio-video system. Drop front panels conceal voluminous storage for tapes as well as a commodious built-in bar; black was chosen as much for its elegant flavor as for the contrast it offers when someone is viewing the television.

The mahogany topped pedestal table easily serves the need of small conferences or in-office lunches; leather covered swivel-mounted chairs allow maximum comfort and mobility. Adequate illumination was provided by recessed ceiling fixtures and an entire wall of butt-joined glass panels—recessed in the valance is a window blind that can be lowered for greater privacy and light control.

Photograph by Jaime Ardiles-Arce

PROJECT DESIGNS

◀ A figured wall of black laminate holds concealed storage as well as a flush-mounted audio-video system. A panel of black grille cloth defines the location of a speaker near the ceiling line; the pedestal table is well suited for business conferences as well as in-office lunches.

MEDIA DESIGN

The interior of the entertaining room features a curved library wall that houses a large television screen (right). An electronically activated panel, simulating booklined shelves (left), rises up out of the floor to mask the screen while the projector simultaneously recedes into the floor, thereby concealing the entire system.

◀ A polished-steel pool table defines the entry into the new entertaining room. Floor-to-ceiling panels open to reveal a complete audio system and ample storage space. Recessed floodlights provide the major source of illumination.

Photographs by Daniel Eifert

Comprehensive Entertainment

Rubén de Saavedra has long avoided an easily recognizable design signature. Instead of creating repetitive interiors, he prefers his work to reflect the taste and awareness of each individual client. Yet there is evidence of a higher order that is clear throughout all of de Saavedra's work: De Saavedra's skillful orchestration of the traditional and the contemporary allows him to venerate the past without reiterat-

PROJECT DESIGNS

ing a set of established design icons. The result is interiors that are referenced with the implication of two eras.

For this extensive project, de Saavedra was charged as both interior designer and architect. Beginning with the newly constructed wing he designed, de Saavedra planned the interior to fulfill any entertainment whim. There is a library, pool table, bar, audio system, and a large-screen projection television. Entering through mirrored doors off the entry foyer, one first sees the polished-steel pool table; covered in russet-colored felt to match the rest of the room, it sets a very relaxed tone.

Cue sticks are rack-mounted on the front of a carpeted storage cabinet, the top of which features two control panels for the telephone, intercom, lighting, and audio systems. On the opposite wall a pair of floor-to-ceiling panel doors opens to reveal a shelf-mounted stereo system. In view of the client's refined taste in audio, the assemblage is impressive: four Sony 4-inch monitors, Audio Control equalizer C22, Sony Betamax, RCA Selectavision videodisc player, Zenith VCR, Surround Sound video processor, Surround Sound amplifier, Kenwood preamplifier M1, ADA sound monitor, a custom switching unit, Pioneer laserdisc, and an RCA compact disc player. Four flush-mounted speakers complete the profile.

Beyond the pool table the main entertaining area is flanked by a commercially equipped bar on one side and a library on the other. Seating in the room is intelligently arranged and comfortable; a custom banquette is supplemented by a pair of swivel-mounted tub chairs. If additional banquette seating is required, two slipper chairs were designed to fit into a niche created by a passageway through the banquette to the bar. Since the clients and their guests enjoy relaxing with their feet up, custom tables were designed with padded leather trim for added comfort.

The curved library—its shelves trimmed in copper with green lacquer inserts—strikes a more traditional note. But this is

MEDIA DESIGN

no ordinary library. The touch of a switch initiates a rather unexpected bit of magic. As the library's midsection (actually a panel fabricated to simulate the surrounding bookshelves) descends into the basement, the television projector simultaneously rises up through the floor. Scrupulous attention to detail embraces the practical as well as the decorative: The television screen is set against a matte black surround for greater picture contrast, while the projector is completely sheathed in polished copper. This package makes the projector appear less obtrusive.

Double-mirrored doors open directly from the media room into the conservatory. A graciously proportioned space immediately adjacent to the living room, it features architectural columns, great arched windows, and a beamed ceiling. Wicker seating from Bielecky Brothers and a nineteenth-century bronze garden sphere uphold the room's more casual outlook. The *pièce de résistance*, however, is a great polished-steel column situated on the back wall. Without a clue as to its functional identity, it actually houses a fully equipped projection room and integrated audio system (a projection port is visible near the top of the column). The column is entered by way of a flush-mounted door—a genius stroke of design integration. The interior of the column is a full 360 degrees; the back half of the column is architecturally extruded through the wall of the house. Considering the scope and complexity of the equipment involved, the system was designed to be completely remote-controlled (one for the audio system and one for the projection system). The equipment profile for this room includes an Automatic Multi-Varactor receiver, a Boulton stereo system master control, two Boulton SX 500 Selectronic control units, Se-Lec-Tronic computer readout, Boulton Selectric turntable, radio master control, tape master control, Nakamichi 700 Tri-Track three-head cassette system, Boulton Selectronic XR/1000 automatic reel tape system, Bell and Howell 16 mm projector, Daylite movie projector screen (8 feet by 8 feet), and six speakers

Photographs by Derrick and Love

◀ A black chaise visually announces a projection television system, its screen cleverly recessed in a custom niche. The projector features custom-designed lacquer panels and a black glass top to conform with the rest of the space.

A built-in cabinet houses ▶ a complete Sony audio system. The newly enclosed foyer features an angled partition and mirrored niche.

Photographs by Peter Vitale

On Symmetry

Designer Kevin Walz used color, furnishings, and simple architectural devices to reiterate a theme of symmetry. Yet the result is not that austere.

Walz bypassed white to create a new harmony of black, gray, blue, and ivory. Though softer and more luxurious, each hue is used with uncanny precision: Matte charcoal columns in the living room impart an air of architectural solidity. Carpeted ledges run the full length of the living room to mock one's perception of the room's narrow width.

Furniture arrangement further reinforces the symmetrical theme—two mirror image groups at either end of the living room with more formal sofas situated by the window. A black chaise consisting of three floor pillows and three back pillows bridges the two living areas and announces a large-screen television. In what could easily have been the "fireplace," Walz mounted the 5-foot screen in a custom niche (proper depth was achieved by borrowing some closet space from the adjoining bedroom). Resembling a coffee table the projector features custom-designed lacquer panels and a black-glass top to conform with the rest of the space. A remote-control panel is mounted on the face of the ledge behind the chaise.

MEDIA DESIGN

◀ A carpeted backrest serves as a picture ledge for a rotating collection of photographs. The television tuner is flush-mounted above a brushed stainless steel telephone panel, custom designed by Patino/Wolf.

Widely spaced ▶
enclosures and reveals
lend architectural clarity to
the media storage system.
Both the turntable and
videocassette recorder are
set on slide-out trays for
ease of operation; slatted
maple table is circa 1954.

Refined Surfaces

The interiors of Bob Patino and Vincent Wolf broadly reconcile the intellectual demands of modernism and the more emotional aspects of living; simple coherent spaces are intelligently planned to match human needs and expectations.

Located in a New York City penthouse, this room is designed to accommodate a variety of activities with calculated luxury and practicality. Replete with leather banquette, book-lined shelves (not shown), and a new entertainment system, it can be used as a secluded retreat or guestroom.

Acute spatial limitations and windowless walls made this room dangerously introspective. Addressing the problem with characteristic restraint, co-designers Patino and Wolf used architectural devices and surface treatments to arouse one's visual instincts: A carpet-wrapped platform, for example, forces the illusion of greater perspective against walls treated with twenty-seven coats of automobile lacquer. With deference to the "form follows function" school of thought, the same carpeted platform is used as a seating strategy and picture ledge.

An integrated audio-video system opposite the banquette permits easy viewing and access. The methodology behind its storage and display, however, is more than just a hackneyed reanalysis of the media cabinet. Fabricated in white-stained and lacquered wood, widely spaced enclosures and reveals imbue the wall with substantial architectural clarity and strength. Matte black audio components—chosen with an eye for aesthetics as well as sonics—are all flush-mounted, as is the 25-inch color video monitor. Slide-out trays accommodate the turntable and videocassette recorder; a drawer provides tape storage.

Full-width recesses across the top of the wall accommodate oversize books as well as one of the room's two speakers; a niche along the bottom accepts the period fifties table for additional space. Chosen by the client, the audio system is largely Yamaha: PX3 turntable, M4 amplifier, T70 tuner, and C4 preamplifier. A Nakamichi 480-2 cassette deck completes the audo profile. Video components include the 25-inch Sony Profeel color video monitor and tuner; speakers are also Sony.

Photographs by Derrick and Love

MEDIA | DESIGN

Photographs by Derrick and Love

Video Dimension

In this New York City library, paneled walls, book-lined shelves, and comfortable furnishings allude to a noble eighteenth-century birthright. More than just reiterating traditional design themes, however, the room acquiesces to the demands of modern living and entertaining. The key is a new entertainment system effectively assimilated with respect to the surrounding space and the owners' wishes.

Russian walnut paneling, commodious seating, and a built-in bar have long made this room a favorite spot for small-scale entertaining. With a taste for video, the owners required a new methodology for storing and viewing their burgeoning videotape collection. Explicit with regard to their needs, the owners specified a functional yet respectful mode of assimilation, a quality system, and ease of operation.

Barbara Ross, ASID, and Barbara Schwartz, ASID, of Dexter Design Inc. addressed the problem with a unique media tower. The key to its success is a design that replicated, line-for-line, the room's original panel molding and its exceptional foliated cornice.

Acknowledging the owners' wish for convenience, open shelves permit easy tape selection and storage, while a pivoting tray for the video monitor eases the viewing angle. A "dead" storage compartment beneath the monitor is concealed behind a hinged panel.

Cliff Shumaker and Hal Pontez, The Audio Consultant, designed and installed a "videocentric" entertainment system for operational ease and quality performance. The equipment profile includes an RCA digital command center, RCA 25-inch color video monitor, and a General Electric 4016 videocassette recorder; Sony speakers mounted in the panel surrounding the VCR were selected as a space-saving measure. A separate audio system (not shown) for background music was shelf-mounted in an existing bookcase. Shumaker and Pontez selected all AIWA micro components in consideration of their listeners' musical expectations and the cabinet's narrow depth. The AIWA system includes a stereo cassette deck DK L80, AM/FM stereo tuner R80, DC power amplifier P80, stereo preamplifier C8, and remote control receiver. A pair of KEF 101 speakers is concealed, one located beneath each lighted vitrine.

◀The new video tower perfectly duplicates the panel molding and foliated cornice of the original walls. A pair of small speakers is flush-mounted in a panel surrounding the videocassette recorder. Silk-shaded floor lamps and complementary tub chairs reiterate the room's traditional symmetry.

◀Seating is comfortable and arranged for easy viewing before a book-lined niche. Audio speakers are hidden in covered wall niches beneath a pair of lighted vitrines (one shown). The pewter sconce is antique Viennese, one of a pair flanking the built-in bar.

Fireplace Perspective

A skylit cathedral ceiling and gracious proportions are the hallmarks of this entertaining room designed by Rita Falkener and Stan Stuetley. Capitalizing on the secluded garden views, they opted for an understated color palette punctuated by simple, yet luxurious, furnishings.

Among the owners' list of essentials were ample storage space and a fully remote audio system. To meet the first criterion Falkener and Steutley specified one entire wall of built-in cabinetry. Installed around an existing fireplace, the cabinet doors appear as fixed-wall panels—a rather lighthearted interpretation of traditional eighteenth-century paneling. Closer examination reveals a series of flush-mounted doors, all of which open by way of pressure-sensitive latches. Fabricated in ash, the wall lends a warm honey-colored glow to the room.

Ron Wellworth of International Audio Company was called in for the audio consultation and installation. After assessing the clients' needs, Wellworth collaborated with the designers on the appropriate cabinet specifications and proceeded to assemble the system. All components are finished in matte black and include the following: Technics SLB5 record changer, TEAC auto-reverse reel-to-reel, North American Phillips tuner, and Soundcraftsmen amplifier with complementary equalizer and preamplifier. Commanding the entire system is a REM 2500 wireless remote-control unit. Programmed to perform thirty-two functions (the unit is capable of 256 functions), some of its features include master volume control, five direct-access preset stations, tune up or tune down for the presets, plus control of every light in the house. Laboratory engineered custom-designed ceiling speakers RSQ8-G (manufactured by ONN ELECTRONICS) are used throughout the house.

▶ A skylit cathedral ceiling adds architectural drama to this entertaining room designed by Rita Falkener and Stan Stuetley. A selection of African artifacts lends a note of ethnicity to this otherwise contemporary space.

Photograph by Daniel Eifert

▶ Ash panels open to reveal a sophisticated audio system housed in the fireplace wall. The large compartment beneath the tape deck permits easy access to the turntable.

PROJECT DESIGNS

Photograph by Derrick and Love

89

Skyline Electronics

Designer Kenneth Brian Walker used a spectacular skyline view as the cornerstone of his design plan for this New York penthouse. Surface treatments and furnishings were all orchestrated to enhance the panorama and bring the view indoors.

Because of limited space in the bedroom, Walker specified a bed with built-in storage, dressing table, and electronic control panel. For added visual interest it was angled at 45 degrees and heightened with a two-step platform. Mirrored closet doors are used to create the illusion of a continuous skyline view along the wall; polished steel ceiling slats, installed at the same angle as the bed, enhance the nighttime glamour while light beige carpeting lends a warm touch amidst the glittering surfaces. The result is truly spectacular.

Speakers, hidden in the radiator convectors, are driven by the main system in the living room and can be controlled from one of the bedside panels. For video, Walker created a niche in the closet wall to house the 25-inch color television, its location perfectly calculated to ensure comfortable viewing from the bed.

Photographs by Jaime Ardiles-Arce

Set in a niche surrounded by mirrored closet doors, the television was carefully placed to ensure maximum comfort while watching from bed.

The custom sofa takes its design cue from the angled living room windows. A centralized audio system provides music throughout the apartment by way of speakers hidden in the radiator enclosures.

MEDIA / DESIGN

Projector Undisguised

An air of sophisticated luxury prevails in this media room by California-based designer, Michael Taylor. While the house features a centralized audio system with control panels in nearly every room, this space was specifically designated for television viewing. Custom-designed sofas and a number of wicker armchairs provide ample and comfortable seating. Nothing spartan about the room, a reflective ceiling heightens the drama while fabric-covered walls add subtle texture and inhibit undue resonance. A Kloss NOVABEAM projection television is the nerve center of the room. While most designers choose to camouflage the projector in a variety of clever ways, Taylor boldly left this one open to full view. And the beauty of it all is the way it unobtrusively blends into the total plan without a trace of compromise.

Left totally untouched, a television projector blends effortlessly into this media room designed by Michael Taylor.

Photograph by Jaime Ardiles-Arce

MEDIA DESIGN

94

PROJECT DESIGNS

◀ A sophisticated array of audio components is flush-mounted along the inside panels of the four-poster bed. Audio Command control panels—each with telephone—are conveniently placed at bedside and adjacent to the leather-covered desk; a custom Plexiglas shower dome stands at the far end of the bed.

Photograph by Phillip H. Ennis Photography

Bedroom Indulgence

When evaluated in the context of electronic technology, Eric Bernard's work is immediate rather than futuristic. His interiors respond with a attitude of compatibility between design and technology that is best described as axiomatic. So strong is this compatibility, in fact, that one is best appreciated in the context of the other.

Bernard approached this project as an artistic rather than decorative commission. The question at hand involved creating an environment that was both an expression of art as well as architecture—one that could fulfill the demands of modern living without obliterating space.

Bernard's solution was a room-within-a-room: Taking substantial cues from the Federal-style paneling, Bernard created a bedroom retreat around his reinterpretation of the traditional four-poster bed. An essay in architectural functionalism, the columns define the space, house every possible amenity, and contain the major lighting elements of the space.

Covered in progressive shades of teal-blue leather (outlined with a black bullnose edging) the "room" assumes varying qualities of light and shadow when viewed from different sides. More importantly, however, each column is appointed to accommodate a variety of particular needs. The columns at the head of the bed, for example, house all the audio components. Flush-mounted along the inside panels, they create a dizzying array of the finest electronics available. A pier bridge between the columns houses a projection screen (lowered into place by a voice-activated mechanism) and a wireless remote control.

The remaining two columns are equipped with different amenities: one houses the icemaker, refrigerator, and bar, while the other is for the computer terminal, telephone, and audio-video control panel by Audio Command. The television projector is pier-mounted between these two columns. The environment is completed with two major appointments at either end of the bed: a Hastings whirlpool with custom plexiglass dome on one end and a leather-covered desk at the other.

Lighting designers Jim Knuckles and Francesca Bevridge devised a simple plan around the architecture of the bed itself; ambient illumination is derived from each of the capitals, while task lighting is by way of recessed fixtures mounted in the piers between the bed columns.

The entire audio-video system was designed and installed by Audio Command and includes the following: Audio Command terminal; Audio Command power supply; Denon POA-1500 power amplifier, PRA-1000 preamplifier, DE-70 equalizer, and TU-750 digital tuner; Akai GXF-44R auto-reverse cassette deck; Teac X1000RB auto-reverse reel-to-reel; Technics SL-10 turntable; Denon DCD-2000 digital audio disc player; Audio Command remote-control panel model #8004/telephone; JVC HR-7650U videocassette recorder; and Braun L-200 speakers.

MEDIA DESIGN

PROJECT DESIGNS

◀ The bed is flanked by a Plexiglas shower dome on the far side and a leather-covered desk/dressing table on the near side. The leather chair with polished steel base was custom-designed by Bernard; sculpture is by Tony Mara.

Hinged panels conceal ▶ hidden storage compartments inside each of the four columns. Access to the shower is either directly from bed or by way of a stepped platform around the Plexiglas dome.

An open side panel ▶ adjacent to the desk reveals a built-in bar and icemaker. Interior lighting is automatically activated when the panel is opened.

Photographs by Peter Paige

MEDIA DESIGN

Sculpted Monolith

If the meaning of luxury has been extended to include tranquillity, Noel Jeffrey's design for this New York apartment is exemplary. Furnishings, color, light, and perspective have been carefully planned to produce a contemplative atmosphere for this urban pied-a-terre.

Jeffrey used a carpeted platform to divide the large room into two distinct areas: a library with grand piano and game table in the back and a seating area with banquette and upholstered chairs in front.

The functional identity of a black monolith is ingeniously concealed behind its architectural façade. Closer inspection, however, shows it to be a cabinet with doors that conceal a built-in bar, voluminous storage space, and some basic video components. Despite its rather imposing dimensions, the cabinet is totally sympathetic with the rest of the room; great rounded corners and a less-than-full-height elevation are the hallmarks of successful integration.

The custom banquette designed by Jeffrey provides ample seating adjacent to the cabinet; tub chairs are swivel-mounted for convenience and mobility. Disappearing pocket doors open to reveal a Zenith 25-inch color television along with an RCA videocassette recorder and Manhattan cable box. A complete Sony audio system is mounted in the bookcase near the piano; there are a total of four speakers in the room, two of which are flush-mounted in the black cabinet.

Photographs by Derrick and Love

◄ The black monolithic cabinet is architecturally sympathetic with the rest of the room. Great rounded sides and a less-than-full-height elevation help scale the unit to size.

Pocket doors open to ► reveal a television, videocassette recorder, and cable box. For added convenience the television is mounted on a pivoting tray; black grille cloths reveal the location of two flush-mounted speakers in the upper corners of the cabinet.

MEDIA DESIGN

100

◀ White lacquer cabinets house audio components flush-mounted along a horizontal surface rather than on the more usual vertical plane. A niche has been carved out of an existing wall to accept the television screen.

Photographs by Jaime Ardiles-Arce

Collaboration in White

The collaborative efforts of two enormously creative minds can more often than not result in unpleasant consequences. Exceptions to this rule, however, can be extraordinary. Consider this apartment designed by Angelo Donghia for a well-known fashion designer. Both in its architecture and decoration the space marks a somewhat radical departure from Donghia's earlier work.

Totally gutted, the apartment was restructured as a vast open space where rooms are merely suggested rather than clearly defined. White walls and furnishings and bare floors easily embrace a new-found feeling of spaciousness. The media room, however, is treated with greater warmth: Of clearly more intimate proportions, it features butterscotch leather sofas and a carpeted floor treatment. Flanking a recessed Advent television screen, custom-made white lacquer cabinets accommodate the room's audio components, storage space, bookshelves, and desk surface.

Because of their shallow depth, the audio components—Yamaha tuner, amplifier, and preamplifier; Teac cassette deck; and Audio Command control panel—were flush-mounted along a horizontal surface. One can simply look down onto the components mounted at desktop height. A fully automatic Bang & Olufsen 4004 turntable sits atop the same surface closest to the screen. Closed storage below houses a Sony VCR, Teac open-reel tape player, as well as records and tapes. A niche with radius corners was carved out of an existing wall to accept the large Advent television screen. The projector and linear control panel are all concealed in the white lacquer coffee table designed by Donghia. Audio-video design and installation is by Audio Command.

The living room of this ▶ large Fifth Avenue apartment designed by Angelo Donghia features a pure architectural approach and uncomplicated furnishings. Upholstered modulars from Angelo Donghia function equally well for intimate conversation or large-scale parties.

PROJECT DESIGNS

MEDIA DESIGN

On Video Conferencing

Handcrafted wood and cabinetry has long suggested a sense of the past. When used in an executive area, it articulates an image of timelessness; the establishment is here to stay.

The newest conference centers throughout the country are acknowledging the potential of video technology by incorporating such electronics into their design plans. The most successful solution not only accommodates the electronic need but will uphold the integrity of the corporate image as well.

One outstanding facility is the executive conference room at the Remington on Post Oak Park in Houston. Designed by Lou Cataffo of Intradesign, Inc., the space conceals all the accouterments of a video theater.

A rose-colored marble conference table sets an obvious note of elegant style for the room; leather covered Queen Anne style chairs suitably complement with formal grace. Fine wood handcrafting is evident in the carved dado that encircles the room while a mohair fabric was used on the walls for the added luxury of soundproofing. It is Catafo's sleight-of-hand with the video components, however, that makes this room a success. What appears to be a paneled wall with beveled mirror insets is actually a series of bifold doors that open to reveal a large projection screen. The projector itself was mounted on the ceiling, well out of the conferees' direct line of vision. Speakers are concealed on either side of the screen behind grille cloth panels.

Photographs by Jaime Ardiles-Arce

◀ *Fine woodworking, Queen Anne style chairs, and a marble table reiterate the traditional atmosphere of this executive conference room. The painting is nineteenth-century English.*

Beveled mirror panels ▶ *above the dado open to reveal a large projection screen. The projector is ceiling-mounted while the speakers are recessed on either side of the screen behind fabric panels.*

MEDIA DESIGN

Deco-Inspired Minimalism

Designer Nicholas Calder upheld the architecture of this suburban New York home with an open, light-filled plan and sparse furnishings. Softening the austerity of his minimal approach is a calculated air of the retrospect; glass-block walls, pipe railings, and Deco-inspired seating recall the nautical motifs of a luxury ocean liner.

The first step in Calder's renovation was gutting the house's public wing. An existing foyer, hallway, and formal dining room were all eliminated. In keeping with his client's wishes, Calder created an intimate dining alcove just outside the kitchen; the area is finished with a banquette and custom laminate table.

The living room was treated with softly curved modular seating. The warm tones of the bare flooring seemingly recall a ship's decking and encourage the seating to be moved as the need arises. To clarify the living room and dining area, Calder designed a free-standing cabinet that also holds a television. A rather inspired design in ivory and black laminate, the counter top and enclosure beneath appear to float between a double row of vertical pipe supports. Its most ingenious quality, however, is the side-mounted panel drawer that slides open to reveal a 25-inch television. Closing the panel hides the unit's dual identity with considerable élan.

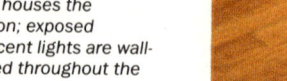

▶ With equal parts of practicality and sleight-of-hand, a panel drawer conceals a television inside the cabinet. The counter top is often used as a bar or buffet when entertaining.

◀ Glass-block windows, white pipe railings, and Deco-inspired seating recall the nautical motifs of a luxury ocean liner. The free-standing cabinet on the left houses the television; exposed fluorescent lights are wall-mounted throughout the space.

Photographs by Ken Spencer

A Private Screening

For this private screening room architect G. Michael Mosteller drew on classical motifs to echo the cues of a 1930s movie palace. Everything was meticulously planned; even the color red was chosen because of its association with grandeur and a "night on the town."

The client for this project was eminently clear as to his needs. A nostalgia buff with an eye for theatrical entertaining, he wanted a suitable room in which to show a growing collection of black-and-white 16 mm vintage films.

Mosteller set the stage perfectly. A curved and mirrored anteroom receives guests and establishes a sense of occasion. To better focus the attention of the viewer, Mosteller forced the illusion of greater perspective by reducing the width of the red panels as they approach the screen. A continuous length of molding interconnects the panels (rather than concentrically repeating the shape of each one) to reiterate the effect. Rheostat-controlled wall sconces are the room's sole source of illumination.

A fluted column designed by Mosteller holds the projector at the appropriate height; pressure-sensitive doors on the column's surface conceal an amplifier, pre-amplifier, and noise reduction unit inside its hollow core. All of the sound in the room is projected through a single speaker flush-mounted in the exaggerated base beneath the screen.

Carpeting, upholstered tub chairs, and curtains provide adequate damping. Richard G. Morris was the project architect, Greta Wail the design assistant, and John Lievsay the sound assistant.

This screening room ▶ epitomizes the ultimate in at-home entertaining. Audio components are shelf-mounted beneath the screen while open shelving on the right is reserved for tape storage. Soundproofing was accomplished with acoustic panels wrapped in fabric.

Photograph by Norman McGrath

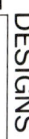

MEDIA DESIGN

▲ The dining alcove is set with a Charles X table and chairs. An original wall sconce and "high tech" floor lamp playfully counterpoint as dual sources of illumination.

Melded influences are clearly demonstrated atop the bedside table where antique bibelots share space with Sony's 3.7-inch Trinitron KV-4100. ▼

Villa Courtyard

A lyrical scene recalling a special moment in time—midnight, perhaps, in an imaginary villa. With an eye for the "ambiguous," designers Allen Scruggs and Douglas Myers have chosen elements for bold contrast and deliberate effect. Their palette of juxtaposing themes mocks our perception of illusion and reality. Never has fantasy been so well calculated.

Though outwardly a bedroom, the space is infinitely more profound. Both indoor and outdoor influences collide with intellectual precision: A tiled reflecting pool, string lights, and crumbling water-stained walls evoke a garden terrace, while fine antiques conjure up a sophisticated salon. The room solicits its very own sense of intrigue.

At the focus of the room is a Beidemeier sleigh bed evocatively tented in "opera net." A dining alcove—appointed with a Charles X table and chairs—is illuminated by an industrial-style floor lamp. Italian floor tile was used for the reflecting pool and floor treatment, softened by the presence of an antique Persian carpet. Walls were treated as great canvases and feature trompe l'oeil stucco "aged" with painted cracks and water stains.

Never shy about contrasting eras, co-designers Scruggs and Myers have perched an advanced 3.7-inch Sony Trinitron color television atop a Charles X side table. The unit features a built-in AM/FM radio, seven AM or FM station memory presets, built-in microcassette recorder, as well as video and audio input jacks. The lighting is by Celeste Gainey.

PROJECT DESIGNS

◀ In the style of a villa courtyard, sleeping, dining, and sitting areas surround a reflecting pool. The very fine Biedermeier bed is shown tented in "opera net," while overhead, a string of World War II "blackout bulbs" provides soft illumination.

Photographs by Keith Scott Morton

MEDIA DESIGN

Photographs by Derrick and Love

PROJECT DESIGNS

▲ A Sony FX-310 provides a more personal approach to audio-video entertainment. The small unit incorporates a television, tape deck, and AM/FM radio. A pair of classic Tizio lamps and a Breuer side chair complete the vignette.

◀ The audio-video system is housed in a cantilevered unit opposite the bed. Drawers provide storage for personal effects as well as for a library of tapes.

Simple Domain

Uncomplicated design solutions demand scrupulous attention to form and function. Spatial volume and structural harmony must be understood as considerations of the highest order. Acknowledging this tenet, designers Scott Bromley and Robin Jacobsen continue to create their successful interiors in the contemporary idiom; the simplicity here is a example.

For this master bedroom—pared down to the bare essentials of a bed, nightstands, and a side chair—the client wanted an integrated storage cabinet for personal use and for the display of his audio-video system. Hampered by the room's somewhat constrained dimensions and minimal ceiling height, the designers opted for a low, multidrawered cabinet to follow an existing L-shaped niche along one wall. For visual relief the cabinet was cantilevered to reduce its mass and lighten its appearance.

Fabricated in mocha-colored laminate, the unit features segments of triple-stacked drawers, a pattern interrupted only by the central media section. The equipment, chosen by the client, includes a Zenith tuner CV512, Zenith amplifier CV520, Zenith Multi-program Source Selector CV540, Zenith 19-inch diagonal high resolution color video monitor CV1952, AIWA stereo integrated amplifier SA-A60H, AIWA cassette deck SD-L50H-C, and an AIWA AM/FM stereo tuner ST-R50U. A pair of Zenith Allegro speakers CV150 are flush-mounted in the cabinet (only one is visible).

111

MEDIA | DESIGN

Tiled for Luxury

Purchased at auction, a collection of blue and gray French ceramic tiles (circa 1920) became the decorative leitmotif of this apartment designed by Eric Bernard. Restructured on a circular plan, tiles were laid in a sunburst pattern radiating out from the centrally carpeted living area; cement between the tiles is painted in a faux granite. A tiled frieze—bordered with brushed stainless steel strips—runs along the perimeter of the entire apartment and appears on the flush-mounted cabinet doors in the dining room. Architecturally reiterating the room's circular plan, a concave partition separates the living area from the distinct dining area.

Seating in the living area is confined to a sweeping banquette designed by Bernard. Covered in a shirred velvet, it warmly counterpoints the mélange of slick surfaces throughout the room and the triple-tiered brushed stainless tables.

A centralized audio system from Audio Command was flush-mounted in the foyer. Audio Command control panels are conveniently placed throughout the apartment while speakers were flush-mounted in the vicinity of the sofa and dining table for optimum sound.

◀ In the image of an architectural canopy, a newly created ceiling cove was silver leafed and edge-lit with pale pink neon. A tile frieze frames an important Henrí Deluermoz painting; the centralized audio system is flush-mounted by the foyer.

The dining area features ▶ a set of matching Josef Hoffmann black lacquer chairs and glass-topped table. An Audio Command control panel is mounted in the surface of the concave partition, which further defines the living and dining areas. The window is covered in stainless steel chain mail.

Photographs by Peter Vitale

MEDIA DESIGN

Photographs by Norman McGrath

Decorative Simplicity

Located on the forty-third floor of the Olympic Tower, this apartment clearly demonstrates a respect for simplicity. Los Angeles-based designer Francisco Kripacz has used minimal furnishings, simple architectural devices, and logical surface treatments to create interior harmony.

The apartment's spectacular view was the cornerstone of Kripacz's design plan. Mirrored walls, unadorned windows, and a glass-tiled floor treatment set the stage with appropriately reflective surfaces. Furnishings have been pared down to the minimum: a velvet-covered modular seating unit and polished steel coffee table. Providing a major source of color in the room, a large Ellsworth Kelly painting—itself a masterpiece of simplicity—hangs on the only bare living room wall.

Essentially an L-shaped layout, the living and dining areas are immediately adjacent to one another. At the juncture of the two spaces a single cabinet—remarkably unobtrusive considering its size—contains an audio-video system. Fabricated in sandblasted aluminum and uncomplicated in design, the unit is effortlessly compatible with the space. A horizontal black band visually scales the cabinet and permits flush-mounted components of varying size to conform with the unit's geometry. Matte black components from SAE include a digital tuner, amplifier, preamplifier/equalizer, and cassette player. A Bang & Olufsen turntable, 19-inch Sony color monitor, Sony Betamax, and a reel-to-reel unit complete the system. A pair of Bose speakers—customized with white lacquer

◀ The media unit stands at the intersection of the living and dining areas. In addition to housing the entertainment system, the cabinet contains storage space for records, tapes, table accessories, and a bar.

◀ The media cabinet features sixteen storage compartments and is finished in sandblasted aluminum. A horizontal black band permits flush-mounted components of varying size to conform with the unit's geometry.

Photographs by Norman McGrath

and grille cloths—are suspended from the living room ceiling; two B & O speakers are mounted in the cabinet.

The hallway leading to the bedroom is lined with mirrored closet doors—a slick visual counterpoint to the medley of warm colors and textures beyond. The beds, conceived by Kripacz as soft boats, rest atop a platform of lacquered parchment. A small "trap door" between them lifts open to reveal a Bang & Olufsen AM/FM tuner, telephone, and wireless remote control.

The focal point of the room is a wall-mounted media/storage cabinet lacquered in ivory. Flush doors conceal personal storage as well as the following equipment: BSR turntable, Sony 19-inch color monitor, a Bang & Olufsen amplifier, and a Sony Betamax unit. Two exposed sections of black grille cloth reveal the location of Bang & Olufsen speakers in the unit's uppermost corners. Attending to even the slightest detail, Kripacz included a flip-down writing surface, interior lighting, and two telephones.

▲ Conceived as soft boats, custom-designed beds sit atop a platform of lacquered parchment. A "trap door" between the beds lifts open to reveal a telephone, AM-FM tuner, and wireless remote control for the television and Betamax.

The ivory lacquer media/▶ storage cabinet in the bedroom houses a television, turntable, amplifier, and Betamax unit. Two panels of black grille cloths reveal the location of the speakers in the unit's uppermost corners.

◀ Mirror panels in the living room reflect a large Ellsworth Kelly painting. A pair of Bose speakers—ceiling-suspended from tube covered chains—have been customized with white lacquer and grille cloths. The coffee table was designed by Joseph D'Urso.

MEDIA DESIGN

Vacation on Video

When the directors of Club Med—a well-known vacation and travel organization—decided to remodel their New York offices, corporate expectations were clear: a clean, contemporary up-scale image that would attract customers with the same outlook. From the outset, it was decided that video would play a major role in the design; with actual footage of various Club Med resorts, the video would be used as an effective selling/training tool.

Acknowledging Club Med's corporate identity, architect Karl Christopher filled the glass-walled foyer with vacation imagery: a double aquarium and palm trees underscore the tropical vacation motif. In the foreground, a segmented leather banquette fronts a travertine marble partition incorporating three flush-mounted color video monitors. Used to lure customers off the street as well as to entertain those in the waiting area, continuous footage of Club Med vacation packages is broadcast throughout the normal business hours.

A screening room is located on the second level; appointed with white canvas folding chairs, the room often doubles for small parties or business conferences. An electronically operated screen can be automatically raised or lowered; a valence keeps it neatly concealed from view when it is not in use.

The main source of illumination is provided by four rows of rheostat-controlled ceiling fixtures. An architectural recess runs around the perimeter of the room at eye level; it provides indirect light during a screening.

PROJECT DESIGNS

◀ *Flush-mounted color video monitors entertain customers in the waiting room at Club Med with footage of the company's resorts. A great double aquarium and palm trees heighten the tropical vacation imagery.*

Appointed with ▶ canvas folding chairs, the second-floor screening room often doubles for parties and business conferences. Speakers are flush-mounted in corner recesses at floor level; lighting is all rheostat-controlled.

Photographs by Norman McGrath

MEDIA
DESIGN

Photographs by Mark Ross

Media Island

The main salon of a Fifth Avenue mansion is the setting for this spectacular room designed by Robert Metzger. Fine antiques, vibrant color, and one-of-a-kind accessories have been orchestrated for incomparable luxury. Yet Metzger thoughtfully avoids the ennui so often associated with such spaces by infusing contemporary accents—most notably, the media island.

The bold and innovative use of color was evidently a major part of the design effort. Variegated shades of mauve highlight the hand-carved boiserie and ornate crown molding while floral upholstered panels dramatize the tall windows. A striped silk from Clarence House covers the upholstered seating while plum-colored suede beautifully accents a pair of armchairs. An array of pastel-colored silk throw pillows and an antique carpet from Doris Blau are softening touches.

In order to scale the room and provide functional compatibility, Metzger divided it into two main areas—one for sitting and the other for entertainment. Marking this delineation is a one-of-a-kind rose lacquered island designed by Dakota Jackson. Configured as great interlocking triangles, the unit is comprised of two upright triangular columns linked by an overhead light bridge. A four-part diamond-shaped convenience surface opens to reveal ample storage, as does the pedestal supporting it. One column houses an array of rather sophisticated components, all with matte black finish. The profile includes a T14 tuner, PA10 preamp, and P10 amplifier all from SAE; a Nakamichi cassette deck, and Bang & Olufsen 3404 turntable. A 15-inch diagonal Sony monitor completes the system. Four Audio Command speakers are built into the upper part of the unit itself—two face the sitting area and the remaining two face the game area. A Karl Springer pool table and goatskin game table from Ron Seff complete this side of the room. An antique Chinese Coromandel screen is mounted directly on the wall to be enjoyed as a delicate painting.

The living area is centered on a large custom glass and brass coffee table also designed by Jackson. A series of glass panels rotate around the central brass pedestal allowing for a variety of configurations and maximum convenience. Voluminous seating and an original marble chimneypiece lend a final note of comfort and grace.

◀ A lacquered entertainment unit was used to separate the game area from the living area. The coffee table features glass segments that rotate 360 degrees; an antique Chinese screen was elevated and mounted directly on the back wall.

◀ Dakota Jackson's media unit lends sculptural clarity amid elegant antiques. The left-hand column provides open shelf storage for the built-in bar while the right-hand column neatly houses the audio and video componentry.

MEDIA DESIGN

Architectural Restraint

The den of architect Calvin Tsao's apartment is an essay in decorative restraint. Partially the result of spatial limitations as well as Tsao's own aesthetic, the room was planned as a statement of architectural functionalism.

Furnishings were chosen with a keen eye for retrospective style; Josef Hoffmann's 'Haus Koller' chair and pair of ebonized stools are outstanding examples. A drawing table, illuminated with a pair of Swedish dentist's lamps, stands behind the sofa.

Rather than create an elaborate media installation, Tsao cleverly made use of an existing closet. The unused space was fitted with a custom-designed gray lacquer cabinet with a gridded storage compartment above. Audio equipment was stacked rather than flush-mounted to anticipate his desire to upgrade the system in the future. The equipment includes a Sony Profeel 25-inch color video monitor, Yamaha Linear Tracking Quartz Lock PX2 turntable, Sony Betamax, Yamaha T2 tuner, Yamaha K960 cassette deck, Yamaha C4 amplifier, and a Yamaha M4 preamplifier. A pair of KES speakers are shelf-mounted in a cabinet along a side wall.

◀ Speakers are shelf-mounted above a white lacquered storage cabinet with contrasting drawer pulls. A Victorian music stand holds a rare first edition before a windowed view.

A gray lacquer media ▶ cabinet occupies the space of a former closet. The lighted cove above the cabinet relieves the feeling of enclosure and heightens the ceiling.

PROJECT DESIGNS

Photographs © 1983 by Paul Warchol

123

MEDIA DESIGN

PROJECT DESIGNS

Classic Rapport

Designer Juan Montoya approached this media/guest room with characteristic insight and simplicity. As a comment on twentieth-century industrial design, the interior clarifies the rapport between technology and classic decorating; the Le Corbusier armchairs, Eileen Gray side table, and large projection television all realize a new visual coincidence.

Undertaken by Montoya in the course of an extensive renovation, this room is located in a spacious home designed by Marcel Breuer. With his own self-imposed standards heightened by the master's unseen presence, Montoya planned every move carefully.

Poised on the brink of austerity, white lacquer walls and charcoal gray carpeting set an appropriate background. An extruded wall of white lacquer cabinetry—rising in elevation to the level of the windows—creates a light-emitting clerestory along the entire width of the room. A General Electric rear projection television—its wood grain veneer covered with five coats of lacquer—was flush-mounted in the center of the cabinet wall. Two sets of door panels flank the television, concealing a bar, audio system, and voluminous storage space. Black leather furnishings were selected with comfort and luxury in mind. Accessories demonstrate Montoya's interest in the Far East and Africa: A seventeenth-century Japanese urn is complemented by the color and texture of a basket from Somalia.

◀ White lacquer cabinetry architecturally reinforces the light-emitting clerestory of this media/guest room. Classic Marcel Breuer armchairs and an Eileen Gray side table counterpoint a seventeenth-century Japanese urn and African basket.

Photograph by Peter Vitale

Industrial Attitudes

Eschewing the anonymous imagery of most contemporary offices, designer Michael McCoy has created a space that recognizes the activities and occupant it harbors. Symbolic gestures are freely used to encourage the executive to identify with the product as well as the management style of the company.

In this suite designed for an aerospace executive, attitudes and materials are pushed to the executive limit—industrial plastic flooring, colored laminate, and lacquered sheet metal all convey the appropriate industrial identity and management style of the company. Adhering to the "machine as office" philosophy, McCoy referenced the space with appropriate industrial cues: a yellow stripe set into a triangular conference table suggests an airport runway while the table itself is reminiscent of an aircraft wing; separating the conference area from the secretarial area is a series of pivoting fins used as a metaphorical air foil; lastly, yellow markings on the floor designate activity zones.

Five perimeter walls enclose the 1,400-square-foot office while four Space Storage units provide a central anchor for the design. In plan, the office consists of four areas of activity: reception, secretarial support, executive offices, and conference room. All the video equipment is stored in one of the four central cabinets and focused toward the white laminate screen on the far wall of the conference area. One of the smaller storage units in the secretarial station was modified to accept a computer and slide-out keyboard.

In one of the office's two conference areas, a great triangular shaped table focuses attention toward a white laminate projection screen. Acoustical panels between the black storage units help dampen the sound; red air foils serve to partition the space.

Photograph by Peter Paige

MEDIA DESIGN

PROJECT DESIGNS

◀ As seen from the reception area, a pair of Space Storage units anchor the main secretarial station. Leather chairs were designed by Eileen Gray.

Aldo van den ▶ Nieuwelaar's Space Storage towers are used throughout the office in varying heights. Located at the secretarial station, this storage unit was modified to accommodate a computer work station; the keyboard is set on a pull-out tray.

Photographs by Peter Paige

MEDIA DESIGN

PROJECT DESIGNS

Enhanced with brass moldings and radius corners, a custom-designed "armoire" at the center of the display wall houses the entertainment system.

◀ *Double sets of bifold doors open to reveal an integrated audio-video system. An open storage system provides easy access to record albums and videocassette tapes.*

Photographs by Derrick and Love

Informal Elegance

An atmosphere of informal elegance prevails in this apartment designed by Carolyn Guttilla. Soft colors and textures—together with luxuriously upholstered seating—were planned for understated comfort and relaxation. Among her clients' requests was a desire for ample space for storage and display of their African artifacts as well as for an integrated audio-video system.

Guttilla translated her client's wishes into a full wall of integrated cabinetry. Divided by use into three main components, adjustable glass shelves provide flattering display space for the clients' collections. Opaque glass panels conceal a soffit of interior lighting. Waist-high cabinets below provide dead storage for larger items.

Radius corners and a double brass molding reiterate the soft lines of an "armoire" at the center of the wall. Double sets of bifold doors open to reveal the entertainment system—a clever strategy that permits each system to be revealed separately when in use. In keeping with another of her clients' requests Guttilla provided open album and tape storage for easy access. Audio components were shelf-mounted, with the turntable occupying a large compartment to accommodate the dust cover in an upright position. The audio equipment includes a VCR Beta SL 2500, Pioneer Quartz automatic turntable PL-7, Pioneer computer-controlled stereo receiver SX7, and Pioneer stereo cassette deck CT-7R.

MEDIA DESIGN

Entertainment Fulfilled

Designer Stephen Mallory effectively uses bold color with dramatic intent. The interior's impact is derived from luxurious seating covered in graduated shades of magenta. Arranged for intimate conversation, the chaise, ottoman, and period armchairs provide adequate flexibility for small-scale entertaining. The moss green walls and floor covering suitably counterpoint the rich magenta hues and deco-style polished steel/brass torchère.

A glittering media cabinet on the opposite wall imbues the space with realistic entertainment potential. Fabricated in the shape of an upright triangle, its surfaces are sheathed in polished stainless steel, bronze plexiglass, and mirrored glass. One of the cabinet's more unique features is the turntable cutout that allows convenient access from two sides.

Together with Mallory, Audio Design Associates designed and installed the audio system. The components all feature solid brass faceplates (except the reel-to-reel, which is gold-plated) and are flush-mounted on an angled panel just beneath the turntable. Open storage on the bottom of the cabinet is for storage. The equipment profile includes a Phase Linear 8000 turntable, ADA tuner FM 600, ADA System 56 for remote switching, Marantz amplifier DC300, Sony auto-reverse reel-to-reel TC758, Dual auto-reverse cassette deck 828. Mounted inside the cabinet (not shown) are an ADA Computer Control Center CC5 and an ADA Line Driver LD6. The System 56 enhances the system with maximum flexibility, permitting music in eight rooms of the house from six different source selections. Four Canton 260s are used in conjunction with a GLS50 subwoofer; two of the speakers are in the media cabinet, two are behind fabric panels on the opposite wall, and the subwoofer is hidden behind a folding screen.

▲ Luxuriously upholstered seating is arranged for intimate conversation. Period armchairs add a traditional note of formality.

PROJECT DESIGNS

◀ A glittering media unit featuring brass-plated audio components is the focal point of this sitting room.

On-Track Video

In nearly all of Juan Montoya's work appointments are pared down to luxurious essentials, orchestrated against a background of architectural simplicity. Visual texture is intelligently provided by a combination of natural materials and surfaces. In this apartment the usual challenge was underscored by a collection of fine art, each piece of which called for a setting of undistracted beauty. To this end Montoya specified a pearl gray color throughout the entire apartment. The master bedroom is completely devoid of art, leaving room instead for a Kloss NOVABEAM projection television and 6-foot diagonal screen. Because of the room's limited dimensions, Montoya mounted the projector on casters and affixed it to a track running parallel to the bed. When the television is not in use, the projector is rolled down toward the opposite wall and stored in its own special niche in the bottom of a closet. Montoya had the panels of the projector lacquered the same pearl gray as the walls, making it sympathetic with the rest of the room.

Mounted on special tracks, this television projector can be wheeled out of sight when not in use. Its panels were lacquered the same pearl gray as the room.

Photograph by Jaime Ardiles-Arce

PROJECT DESIGNS

DESIGN

Contemporary Details

The interiors of Gwathmey Siegel resonate with a style and quality seldom encountered in the contemporary idiom. Unusual colors, surprising materials, and meticulous detail are all calculated for effect and impact. Nothing is left to chance.

The interior of this New York City apartment was entirely gutted and restructured along the lines of the original plan. Newly installed structural sections correspond to a series of multipurpose internal zones. A polished marble floor treatment dramatically sets the stage.

The living room, den, and dining room are planned as a sequential public space; a wall of white oak cabinetry is all that separates the dining room from the den and adjacent living room. An audio system has been discreetly flush-mounted in one panel of the cabinet facing the den. The matte black components, which can be activated by wireless remote control, also drive speakers throughout the apartment. A fabric panel running along the top of the cabinet conceals the den's speakers. An antique Persian carpet sets off the sparse yet luxurious furnishings: a pair of leather chairs, a drum table, and the cantilevered desk by the window. Columns along the window, covered in brushed stainless steel, add a sophisticated touch.

The master bedroom is similarly sparse yet luxurious. White oak is again used, this time to cover the bed niche and for the nightstands, bookcase, and low cabinet opposite the bed. The room's audio-video requirements are rather simply fulfilled: Speakers are concealed behind a fabric panel in the soffit over the bed and the television was housed in a pivoting lacquer "box." A remote-control panel is built into the angled nightstand beside the bed. The audio-video system was designed and installed by Stratos Hi-Fi.

▲ Luxurious materials are the hallmark of the master bedroom. The television was simply housed in a pivoting gray lacquer "box" set atop a low oak cabinet.

◄ A painting by Magritte lends a note of the surreal to this otherwise contemporary setting.

PROJECT DESIGNS

◀ Matte black audio components are flush-mounted in a wall of custom-designed white oak cabinetry. Speakers are hidden behind a fabric panel along the top; columns by the window are covered in brushed stainless steel.

Photographs by Norman McGrath

MEDIA DESIGN

◀ Bi-fold doors on the mirrored cabinet open to reveal a large projection television screen against a black surround. The column on the left contains a bar; the column to the right of the screen contains one of the room's seven-foot speakers.

Matte black audio ▶ components are flush-mounted along a horizontal plane as a space-saving measure. Elevated to the same height as the desk, the system is easily accessible when a person is seated on either side.

Multifunctioned Retreat

A multifunctional space is intended to fulfill a variety of purposes with equal assurance; ideally, no *one* activity should dominate the room's visual identity. Designed by Tony Antine and Mark Polo, this space perfectly meets the criteria; within these walls, a personal library, art gallery, and media room all coexist with complete design integrity.

By enclosing a pair of the client's existing speakers (each one measuring 6 feet 8 inches by 24 inches) in brushed stainless columns, the co-designers established the architectural leitmotif of the room. Six columns were used to anchor the design, each with a separate functional identity: In addition to the two speaker enclosures, a third column contains a complete bar, while the remaining three are for storage.

A custom-mirrored cabinet is the focal point of the entire room. A pair of centrally placed bi-fold doors opens to reveal a large projection television screen mounted against a black surround for enhanced contrast. Encased in a gray lacquer cabinet and fitted with a polished granite top, the projector sits across from the screen between a pair cashmere upholstered modulars.

Gray, lacquered shelving provides voluminous storage for books and files in front of which the client has chosen to display a portion of his art collection. A custom-made desk, designed by Antine and Polo, features a polished granite top and curved outside edge; matte black audio components were mounted in the cabinetry on a continuous level with the desk.

As a space-saving measure, the components were flush-mounted along a horizontal rather than a vertical plane, making them conveniently accessible when a person is seated nearby. The audio-video design and installation was by Art Powers, Designed Sound.

Photographs by Peter Paige

MEDIA DESIGN

Kitchen Entertainment

With its architectural approach underscored by unusual materials and a complete home-entertainment system, this space best exemplifies a relaxed contemporary lifestyle. Designed by Rita Falkener and Stan Stuetley, the room was planned with entertaining and easy maintenance in mind. Generous use of Italian ceramic tiles lends subtle pattern and texture as a floor treatment throughout; in the foyer the tiles were used on the walls and floor. The modular grid motif is repeated in a grid support over the work counter as well as in the kitchen cabinets. Since cocktail parties take precedence over formal dinners, the dining area was kept intentionally small.

Since the family also planned to spend the majority of their time here, a complete entertainment system was considered essential. Co-principals Falkener and Stuetley used open ash columns to both scale the room and showcase the media equipment. Their rather unusual design visually reduces their mass, making the columns appear lighter and more graceful. All the audio components are shelf-mounted in one column; the other column holds the monitor. The equipment profile—all of which are manufactured by Sony—includes: amplifier TA-AX5, tuner ST-JX5, turntable PS-FL5, tape deck TC-FX7, speakers SS-U80, Profeel monitor KX-2501, video tuner VTX-1000R, Betamax SL-2500, and Profeel monitor KX-1901 (foyer).

Photograph by Daniel Eifert

◀ A 19-inch Sony monitor whimsically emulates fine art atop the foyer pedestal. The tapestry is by Judith Toxson Fawkes, the vase by Mimi Okino.

▲ The monitor is mounted on a swivel tray to allow for convenient viewing while diners are seated around the table. Josef Hoffmann's "Fledermaus" chairs in ebonized beechwood provide a classic touch.

Planned with practicality ▶ and entertainment in mind, a pair of custom-made ash columns showcase a complete home-entertainment system. Four speakers are concealed in soffits above the kitchen and seating area, respectively. Diners can choose between a view of the window or the monitor.

Photographs (middle and above) by David A. Buxbaum

MEDIA DESIGN

Flush-mounted within an existing structural column a series of audio-video components blends effortlessly into Marcel Bredos's design scheme. ▶

Hi-Tech Column

Designer Marcel Bredos set leather upholstered seating and polished steel and glass accents against a background of deep gray in this home office/living room. The combination sets the perfect stage for an integrated audio video system that neither dominates nor retreats within the confines of the space. Rather than specifying new cabinetry, Bredos flush mounted all the components within an existing structural column. The uppermost Pioneer RT-707 reel-to-reel features automatic reverse and provides the major source of music in the room alternating with a Sansui cassette deck just beneath it. Power is supplied by an SAE MK-XXX preamp with a 2200 power amplifier. Several sets of Acoustic Research MS-1 minispeakers were used. Bass is provided by a single M&K subwoofer.

An intimate dining area with mirrored bar is situated in the foyer of the space. A polished aluminum grid sets the illusion of a dropped ceiling without sacrificing the feeling of spaciousness. ▼

Photographs by Jaime Ardiles-Arce

MEDIA | DESIGN

A low partition visually defines the newly created foyer. Mirror panels amplify the space, while ceiling soffits hold recessed light fixtures and add architectural interest; the custom coffee table is travertine marble.

Armoire Audio

Designers Bob Patino and Vincent Wolf used simple architectural devices to clarify this formerly undistinguished apartment. Ceiling soffits, partitions, and built-in furnishings add structural definition while visually enhancing the space. Acknowledging the client's request for a pastel environment, colors were intentionally restricted to shades of lavender highlighted with polished brass and steel.

A low partition was used to suggest a foyer and more formally define the living area; an L-shaped banquette allows for maximum seating capacity and comfort in front of this newly allotted space. Leather covered Brno chairs provide additional seating flexibility while the travertine marble coffee table adds a note of rough-hewn texture.

As an architectural/decorative solution for separating the living and dining areas, co-designers Patino and Wolf designed an armoire with storage capacity on both sides; lacquered in burgundy, it practically accommodates a variety of storage needs in addition to its obvious role as room divider. Completely lined in mirror, the living room side holds crystal, a bar, and a shelf-mounted micro-series audio system. The opposite side, also fitted with doors, holds table linens and a silver collection. For added convenience, interior lighting in the armoire is automatically activated when the doors are opened.

PROJECT DESIGNS

◀ Completely lined in mirrored glass, the burgundy lacquered cabinet features glass shelves and interior lighting. Audio components are shelf-mounted beneath a pair of storage drawers. Steel framed Brno chairs are covered in mauve leather.

Photographs by Peter Vitale

MEDIA DESIGN

Four-Station Video

Bold use of color makes for a distinctive video/living room by Chicago designer David Snyder. White, chalk-painted walls and ceiling reflect the deep red floor, treated to eight coats of lacquer and polyurethane sealer. Snyder designed the sectional seating with asymmetric backrests and placed them along the outer edge of the room. The arrangement facilitates comfortable television viewing as well as large-scale entertaining.

For the ultimate in home entertainment Snyder has designed this 360-degree four-station video unit. Housed within a black lacquer table measuring 70 inches across and 30 inches high, four RCA televisions (VJM 2023 Digital Command) permit simultaneous yet independent viewing from any angle in the room. Each of the four screens may be used with earphones for tuning into four different programs, video games, sporting events, or whatever else is desired. A Sony Betamax SL 2405 completes the video profile.

Housed in a black ▶ lacquer table, this 360-degree, four-station video system permits viewing from any angle in the room. Individual earphones and Sony Betamax unit increase the system's flexibility.

Photograph © by Hedrich Blessing

Design Basics

Planning is the key to a successful home entertainment system. The room's sonic integrity and visual aesthetic become a measure of balanced design and electronics. Whatever equipment is installed, the success of a system is ultimately how comfortable you feel using it. This success is dependent upon a set of critical variables, all of which are functions of *product awareness, needs, feasibility,* and *execution.* Product awareness is dependent on understanding the media basics (see Chapter 2). The last three variables are more closely related to a person's lifestyle. Needs are determined by such issues as income, interests, and social stature. Musical tastes and equipment expectations must also be considered: The status of the listener must be judged as "critical" or "background," while a compromise must also be reached between the importance of the aesthetics of an entertainment center and its sonic integrity. Resolving this conflict will become the foundation—the elements of design—of a successful entertainment system.

MEDIA DESIGN

Sound Reproduction

Simply stated, sounds are produced by mechanical vibrations. A vibrating object disturbs the molecules of air surrounding it, causing periodic variations in the air pressure. As the object vibrates back and forth, the pressure becomes alternately more, and then less, dense. These pressure variations radiate away from the object, eventually reaching the listener's ear, causing the sensation we know as sound.

It is the constant aim of all true high-fidelity enthusiasts to achieve the ultimate in sound reproduction. The ultimate has not yet been achieved, and it is extremely unlikely that it ever will be. Nevertheless, it is certainly possible to approach very closely in one's own listening space the sound of a concert hall—from a subjective point of view. Like the other senses, hearing is a subjective experience; and the way we hear a piece of music is closely interwoven with the laws of physics. When sound is reproduced by way of loudspeakers, the experience is then also influenced by various laws of electronics and electromechanics.

The Listening Room

The listening room is part of the audio chain between the loudspeakers and your ears; every sound that reaches you must pass through the room and be altered by it. In addition to the room's structural configuration, it is the proportion of reflective to absorptive surfaces that will most affect the sound. It should be no surprise that your choice of a room may have more influence on the final sound than your choice of loudspeakers. For this reason the room itself becomes a component; in most cases, unfortunately, it is the one that is the most usually forgotten.

Like any component, a listening room must have a reasonably flat frequency response in order to avoid screechy highs or boomy lows. Then, too, it must be free of distortion in a physical sense to avoid buzzing or rattling. There are, however, "ideal" parameters to be considered in choosing a listening space or in adjusting the behavior of one already in use:
1. choose an irregularly shaped room
2. use sound-absorbing decor
3. heed speaker manufacturer's positioning advice
4. scatter additional absorbers about
5. provide sufficient amplifier power
6. judge woofer-to-boundary distance carefully
7. judiciously use tone controls and equalizers.

THE AUDIO-VIDEO CONSULTANT

As a liaison between the consumer, the designer, and the new technology, the audio-video consultant understands the complexities of this technology and ensures that a system will be most suited to the listening and viewing needs of his client as well as to the space itself. A full-service consultant will analyze the listening room(s), aid in the selection and design of the system, and fully install it. Analysis of an existing space includes an acoustical as well as an electrical evaluation. Problems are carefully outlined and the most preferable solutions offered. In projects involving any structural changes the consultant is best engaged at the very outset. This is the most cost-effective method, intelligently avoiding unnecessary construction or damaging additional construction. Collaboration between the architect and audio consultant is, of course, ideal in situations where new construction is planned, enabling the perfect listening/viewing room to be built. With the aid of the professional consultant, system types and component selection is undertaken based on the client's needs and feasibility of the space. The consultant will then create a design plan for the physical configuration of the equipment. Finally, he will install and wire all the components, wrapping up the process with a testing and debugging session. In effect, the audio-video consultant ensures the successful articulation of a home-entertainment system.

■ THE SHAPE OF THE ROOM

In the strictest sense, sound is projected and dispersed into the listening room in such a way as to approximate the live performance of the event—the musical sounds and the acoustic atmosphere. From an audio standpoint only, the listening room is the enclosure containing the loudspeakers, which ideally introduce as little coloration as possible on the reproduced sound. In reality, however, some coloration is inevitable because the room acts as a resonator at certain frequencies, governed by its dimensions, thereby amplifying the sound at those frequencies. The acoustic atmosphere of the room should not intrude unduly on the reproduced acoustic atmosphere of the concert hall. A damping effect on the resonances, which is inherently imposed by the furnishings—like carpets and drapes—helps to achieve the integrity of the concert hall. But it is the configuration of the room itself that first deserves your attention.

When a source of sound transfers its output into a closed space, the sound waves are reflected throughout that space by the boundaries of its walls, floor, and ceiling. Those frequencies whose wavelengths fit most neatly into the dimensions of the space are called natural frequencies of the room and constitute its natural "modes" of vibration.

The number of modes to be found in a space of any given dimensions depends essentially on the volume of the room. Thus, a nonrectangular space has as many modes as a rectangular one of similar volume. But these modes of vibration are distributed in a more complex way in an irregularly shaped space, and the fact that they are less likely to coincide (and thus doubly and triply reinforce certain frequencies) in nonrectangular rooms makes this type of space particularly advantageous.

In general, an irregular room shape creates less reinforcement at the natural frequencies; it effectively broadens the tuning of the room modes and makes them more likely to coalesce than they would in a room with a regular shape.

Random placement of absorptive furnishings and the shape of the reflected and absorptive surfaces (shape of the room) contribute to the diffuseness of the reflected sound. The sound ambiance of an especially large room requires even greater attention. For this large New York salon, designer Michael de Santis preserved sonic integrity with carefully placed sound-absorbing furnishings and a carpeted floor treatment.

DESIGN

■ SOUND-ABSORBING DECOR

Absorption at high frequencies is easily accommodated by such strategically placed furnishings as rugs, wall hangings, and upholstered pieces. Experts agree, however, that absorptive material is far more effective when it is distributed randomly throughout a space rather than concentrated in one area. The "critical" listener will want to experiment to come up with the most suitable arrangement.

Random placement of absorptive furniture and the shape of the absorptive and reflective surfaces (as with an irregularly shaped room) also contribute to the diffuseness of the reflected sound. This simply means that sound bouncing off the walls tends to reach the listening area approximately equally from all directions. Despite the advantages in making a listening room highly absorptive, there are disadvantages. A stereo system playing in an absorptive or "dead" space will not sound as loud as one playing in a reflective or "live" space, where the reverberation reinforces the direct sound from the speakers. The acoustics of a dead room may also be found to be dull and unpleasant.

When the loudspeakers are operated at a high volume on its bass frequencies on an uncarpeted wooden floor, the speakers can transfer vibration to the floor, which is another source of coloration called forced vibration. Well-made speaker enclosures should, of course, be free from vibration. The effect can be more severe when some part of the floor structure has a natural resonance frequency within the reproducing range of the loudspeakers. This usually happens at very low bass frequencies; when the frequency corresponding to the resonance sounds, the whole floor vibrates and can often be felt by the listener.

This effect can be reduced by standing the speakers on sound-damping material to reduce coupling to the floor, particularly if the floors are uncarpeted. Although carpeted floors are more damped than uncarpeted ones, so that resonances are better tamed, resonances within and beneath the floor can also occur. To ameliorate this problem, elevating floor-type loudspeakers—usually in keeping with the manufacturer's recommendations—will help. An alternative is to mount the speakers on the wall, for which various types of specific brackets are available (see pages 154 to 155).

■ SOUNDPROOFING AND DAMPING

Although soundproofing is a matter in the realm of personal taste, certain practical advantages from soundproofing and damping ensue even when the room is not being used for music: The level of noise, whether generated internally or externally, is lower; less sound leaks out of the room; two or more conversations can take place simultaneously with reduced aural competition; and the overall acoustics tend to be more intimate, favoring sounds that originate nearby over those from far away.

As mentioned earlier in this chapter, damping (with furniture, carpeting, drapes, objects, etc.) is one technique for correcting the acoustic anomalies of the listening room. Another remedial measure is to make use of a deadening wall—usually either fiberglass or polyurethane—in a fiberglass wall treatment.

A semirigid material, the fiberglass is available in two-foot by five-foot sheets in a one-inch, two-inch, or three-inch thickness. Characterized by an almost ninety-one percent absorption coefficient, it can successfully cope with most of the frequencies in the room and can deaden it considerably.

Installation is best left to the professional builder or contractor, as the fiberglass must be fitted between the interior sheetrock and the exterior wall. Special "spikes" are available that make installation more convenient. Manufactured in different lengths, the spikes are fixed to the wall at intervals by means of a self-sticking base; the batts of fiberglass are then impaled on the spikes.

Three-quarter furring strips can also be used to mount the fiberglass, with the added advantage of dead-air space behind the batt, which helps the absorption. The batts are easily cut to various sizes and shapes for appropriate placement. The room should then be reanalyzed, and the final amount of fiberglass to be added should be determined by the results.

Although every room will be different, there are some rules to guide the fiberglass application process. In a rectangular room, one long wall should be covered with fiberglass and the opposite wall uncovered, unless the modes and reverberation in the room are very pronounced. The material is usually applied on the wall opposite the speakers; if a permanent quadrophonic speaker setup is used, then the fiberglass should be placed on the facing wall as well.

Another material that can be used for soundproofing is Soundfoam. A polyurethane material, it comes in two-foot by four-foot panels, with self-adhesive backing, and in thicknesses of up to one inch. Soundfoam is also available with an embossed pattern and comes in various colors. There is also a special version that features a layer of lead sandwiched between the foam, which acts as a barrier against transmission as well as a deadening material. Soundfoam is ideally suited to curtail musical transmissions between apartments as well as between adjacent rooms in the same household. Although the bass frequencies will still be transmitted through the floor and the adjacent studs, the Soundfoam is approximately

---

PSYCHOACOUSTICAL DISORIENTATION

There is a psychological element in recreating the sound stage—an inroad to the subjective domain of sound. Psychoacoustical disorientation is simply the inability to perceive the reproduced sound as a realistic presentation. It is a function of the listening room, speaker placement, and type of speaker used. A room that is either too dead or too bright will result in a distorted sensation. Placing both speakers on the wall adjacent to the listener or on the same wall behind the listener will produce the disorientation. And, an improperly chosen electrostatic or planar speaker can inflate the image too greatly, while a minispeaker will project an overly diminished image.

seventy-five percent as efficient as the fiberglass. Soundfoam, however, is more costly.

■ SPEAKER PLACEMENT

Part of the strategy in planning an acoustically efficient room directly involves the loudspeakers. And this in turn is dependent upon their design and placement—and on proper amplification. In considering speaker placement, the most important ground rule is that speakers should radiate their sound from an acoustically "hard" surrounding to a more absorptive and sound dispersing part of the room. Acoustically hard surfaces include smooth walls and windows. Upholstered furnishings, carpets, and drapes, on the other hand, will all have a damping effect, while irregular and recessed surfaces will aid in dispersing the sound. The furnishings should be neither too reverberant nor too inert.

At low frequencies, a speaker acts as an omnidirectional sounding source. As the frequency is increased, however, most of the energy is radiated into the listening space, making the speaker more directional. A speaker's bass performance is affected by its position in relation to the walls and floor and the angles formed. With the speaker placed on the floor near a wall, the low frequency (omnidirectional) sounds are reflected back into the room from the two surfaces of the wall and the floor. The effect is an apparent increase in bass output. The bass is also enhanced when the speaker is placed in a corner of the room, which provides three intersecting surfaces to further increase the sound projection. Roughly, bass emission is four times greater when the speaker is located in a corner and two times greater when standing on the floor close to a wall. Conversely, the bass is weakest when the speaker is placed at a distance from both the floor and the side and rear walls.

Another general rule to consider in speaker placement is the farther a listener is from the speakers, the greater the distance should be between the left and right speaker; this is the so-called bass width. For good stereo imagery, a well-known rule of thumb recommends that the two speakers and the listener should form an equilateral triangle. Often, however, a smaller bass width will yield better results. Although a common position for the two speakers in a long room is on either side of a short wall, this is not the best place for them. Significantly less "boom" may result by placing the pair along the long walls not too close to the short walls and not directly across from each other. While this may reduce the effective listening area, it can lead to less colored reproduction and a cleaner, tighter bass. In special cases, such as an L-shaped room, a kitty-corner setup may be advantageous.

As mentioned earlier, taming the acoustic effects at a low frequency involves not the room modes but the distance between the sources of bass sound (woofer cones) and the room boundaries. The sound radiates equally in all directions, reflects from the nearest boundaries, and returns to the woofer.

Most loudspeakers are designed in the form of a "box," with the drivers arranged on one of the long faces of the shape. It is difficult to place the speakers so that the woofer is in suitable proximity to the floor and nearest wall without angling the more directional output of the speaker (the tweeter) away from the listening location. Experience has proven that speakers perform best when located away from the nearest room boundary. It is important to remember that the speaker must be moved away from the floor or ceiling as well as from the walls, which often necessitates placing the speaker on a stand or suspending it.

Following the manufacturer's specifications, you may find it best to mount the speakers on a wall or place them on a table or shelf. For wall mounting, the speakers will have holes drilled in their rear walls; the speakers can usually be pushed directly onto pegs or nails, although a drilling template is recommended so that the screws may be affixed to the wall precisely and without difficulty. When fitted into shelf units or cabinets, the front of the speaker should not stand beyond the front edge of the shelf on which it is placed. Care should also be taken to avoid placing the speakers

Located away from the room's nearest boundaries, speakers are flush-mounted at ear level in a black storage cabinet. The cabinet separates the public and private zones of the apartment. Interior design by Bray-Schaible Design, Inc.

DESIGN

near items that are prone to vibration and resonances. Ideally, the speaker should come right to the top of the shelf space and be flanked on either side—by books, for example. These precautions help prevent resonance from forming in a partly open space around the speaker, which could distort the sound.

Optimal speaker placement is ear level to the seated listener, with both speakers elevated to the same height. The general rule governing placement is to make sure that absolutely nothing comes between the loudspeakers and the listeners to impede or influence sound dispersion. With floor-standing speakers, their elevation with respect to the furniture must be sufficient to provide an unobstructed path to the listeners. This is particularly important for the top half of each speaker, where the treble and midrange units are located, since the sound from these units is more directional than from the bass unit. Since the bass unit is located at the bottom half of the speaker and is essentially omnidirectional, some screening by objects or furniture presents less of a problem. Relatively short or small speakers should be elevated or placed on a stand or table for the best sound.

■ CONFIGURATION AND MOUNTING

The actual display of the audio and video components—their method of arrangement and their relation to each other—figures prominently into the design of an entertainment system. Both variables must be evaluated in terms of the user's visual aesthetics versus musical taste in order to maximize both the components' performances and the user's enjoyment. Components can be displayed in three ways: flush-mounted, rack-mounted, and shelf-mounted. While performance is relatively the same with all three methods, there are some advantages—both cosmetic as well as practical—of one method over another.

Flush-mounting is a cosmetic treatment in which the front panel (faceplate) of the component is flush with its harboring or

In a flush-mounted system, the component's faceplates are set flush with their harboring or adjacent surfaces. These systems are best accommodated in a custom cabinet or nonstructural interior surface.

adjacent surface. It is the most professional-looking technique from a design point of view. Wires are conveniently concealed behind the front panel, leaving only the faceplates of the audio components or the screen of the monitor exposed. The disadvantages with this type of mounting—although ultimately reconcilable—present some very real problems: Because the cabinetry must be reassembled and redesigned each time a new component is added, it can be difficult to upgrade the system; there is inhibited ventilation; and the components are difficult to service because there is limited access.

The upgrading impedance problem can potentially be resolved by using a modular approach to the cabinetry supporting the components. The front panel, for example, should be easily removed with screws or clamps. Initially this means the original panel must be removed and a new panel custom-ordered and cut to fit the new or additional components. This involves both cabinet work and new installation and hook up. This becomes even more costly if rare or exotic materials have been used for the cabinetry.

The inhibited ventilation problem can be alleviated by creating a "bottom-to-top" circulation column. This can be accomplished with louvers, grilles, or ventilating holes at the bottom and top of the cabinet. If a freestanding column is used, a back panel can be hinged for access. However, the heat generated by some Class A amplifiers, regardless of the power capacity, may require a mechanical air circulator or fan to be placed behind the front panel of cabinetry (usually a 3½-inch diameter blower is sufficient). Provisions should also be made to facilitate removal of separate components; lining the bottom of each component with a low-resistance fabric may make removal easier.

Flush-mounting a speaker involves recessing it into a wall or soffit or ceiling so as to enclose five of its six sides. Only the front will remain exposed, flush with the harboring surface so that the grille cloth will be perfectly confluent with the wall or ceiling. This method is suitable only for electrodynamic transducers. Special "flush-mount" speakers, made specifically for this type of display, feature a front baffle, drivers, and a crossover network but no back—instead, the inside of the wall is the enclosure. All that is visible are two circles for each speaker—the larger woofer and a smaller tweeter. While this is easily the sleekest technique, it is the one that presents the most difficulty in terms of servicing because of its limited access.

A dynamic speaker must be fastened to a rigid, nonvibrating surface to counteract any structure-borne resonance. A common technique is to construct a wooden sleeve in the wall that would snugly accept the entire speaker. This helps eliminate resonance by virtually eliminating any closed volumes of air. The sleeve should also be lined with foam—if not on all sides, at least

DESIGN BASICS

In a rack-mounted audio system, specially modified components are held between parallel tracks by means of special brackets. System design and installation by Audio Command.

on the bottom surface on which the speaker is resting. The speaker can then slide into place, the rough wall surface finished and the grille attached.

It should also be mentioned that when mounting a turntable, a recess must be constructed that is not only wide enough to hold the component but also high enough to allow the dust cover to be raised and remain open. Some front-loading and vertical turntables are available, which permit flush-mounting, thereby eliminating the problem. The same holds true for videodisc, VCR, and compact disc equipment; they all must be front-loading models in order to be flush-mounted.

Components may also be **rack-mounted.** In this case, two parallel tracks, placed a standard nineteen inches apart, accept special components by means of angle irons on each side of the component. This type of application is, for example, suitable for a niche that has no shelves; the components would almost appear to float. The advantages here are good ventilation, since there are no shelves, and easy upgrading, since the components are standardized to fit into a rack mount. This standardization can also be a disadvantage, as your component choices are limited to rack-mounting components, which all manufacturers do not make. Rack-mounting can also be freestanding or can support the components with a flush-mounted look. In the latter case, the tracks are mounted inside the cabinetry, bolted in place and the flush panel fitted on last. This method is recommended, since once again there are no shelves to impede ventilation and the wires are most easily concealed from view.

Shelf-mounting is somewhat self-explanatory and by far the most common method of display. In this case the components are merely placed on a shelving system of adequate proportions to hold them in place. Adjustable shelves offer the greatest degree of flexibility. Shelf-mounting is the easiest to set up, service, and upgrade, but it is also the least attractive and presents problems with concealing the wires.

A shelf-mounted entertainment center offers the greatest opportunity for upgrading components. For a more sophisticated appearance, designer Juan Montoya concealed this system behind mirror panels inside a former closet.

For shelf-mounting a speaker, place rubber, felt, or a three-quarter-inch foam pad under the speaker. It is also recommended to surround the speakers with books (see "Soundproofing and Damping") to eliminate any further possibility of resonance. Placement should be anywhere from three to four feet from the floor, depending on what the ear level of the seated listener is intended to be.

For both the conventional flush-mounting system and the shelf-mounting system, a series of horizontal and vertical planes are supporting the components. For ideal performance these shelves are best fabricated in a wood and steel combination. The situation becomes critical, however, when considering the turntable, which must be damped as well as insulated from unnecessary motion and vibration. Damping can be accomplished with the use of lead, slate, or dense wood, while insulation uses lightweight foam or springs. Ideally, the turntable should sit on a shelf of three-quarter-inch plywood. This should, in turn, be covered with a three-quarter-inch multicellular foam layer, which should be covered by a piece of slate which itself makes no contact with the side surfaces.

Configuration of the components and the relative effects of their proximity to each other become an important issue with the increased popularity of flush-mounting. When designing a fully integrated audio-video system, the placement of the television or monitor is most crucial, followed by speaker placement, amplifier placement, and seating arrangement.

Of the audio components, the main culprit is the amplifier; the problem manifests itself as an audible "hum." Amplifiers have large transformers that radiate heat as well as a magnetic field.

Other components operating on magnetic principles, such as recorders (both open reel and cassette) and turntables, should be isolated from the amplifier. Never place a recorder on top of an amplifier, as the tapes could become reoriented or even erased. Turntables placed too near an amplifier will be subject to structure-borne vibration and will project what is best described as a "howl." Furthermore, since the other components are not designed to run hot, the heat generated by the amplifier will wear down these other components. And last, if it is aesthetically desirable or more convenient in terms of available space to stack components, it is advisable to place the amplifier on the very top of the grouping, in that it is the "hottest" element and will thus not affect the components below it (as heat rises).

In the video domain the main problem is positioning the speakers too close to the monitor. Since woofers have their own magnetic field, extending outside the boundary of the speaker itself, it can cause distortion in the video picture. A rule of thumb to follow to prevent distortion is to keep the speakers three feet away from either side of the monitor. There are, however, specially shielded speakers that can be used in close proximity to a monitor. The height of the monitor is also critical to comfortable viewing and should be anywhere from three to four feet from the floor to the center of the screen for the seated viewer. If the viewer is in bed or in a semireclining position, the monitor should be raised. The height, therefore, is dependent on personal taste, function, and use.

A recommended, vertically integrated audio-video system might include the following with adjustments made according to personal taste and ease of operation:

amplifier
tuner
equalizer
preamplifier
cassette deck (or open reel recorder)
compact disc player
turntable
monitor
videodisc
videocassette recorder
television tuner

This list is used more as a frame of reference than for an actual plan. A popular method is to separate the audio components from the video components.

Component Selection

Component selection is one of the most basic elements in the design of an entertainment system. The personal needs and expectations of the viewer/listener as well as the characteristics of the room itself are the determining factors. For video components, selection should be guided by individual projection needs, lighting, and room dimensions. In the audio domain, it becomes crucial to determine the listener's status. Is the user a critical or background listener? Critical listeners will, for example, place acoustic integrity and component performance above all else, opting for a combination of hardware based on purity and efficiency.

■ DISCRETE VS. CENTRALIZED SYSTEMS

The relative importance of an audio-video system and the planned extent of its use will determine not only the choice of individual components but the type of system desired. This translates into a choice between a discrete system or a centralized one. The decision should be based on individual needs, but aesthetic considerations can also figure prominently since the performance of the two systems is relatively equal.

A **discrete system** is one in which there is a separate audio, video, or combined audio-video system for each desired location. Each of the designated rooms has its own self-contained system in no way connected to the system of any other room. The fundamentals of the system are determined by the occupant and/or function of the space. This system provides all the flexibility of a multiroom system but without the room-to-room integration. Other advantages over a central system include easier and less costly installation while allowing for greater individual choice. The system's major disadvantages are duplication of signal/program sources; more costly upgrading, again because of dupli-

DESIGN BASICS

With a discrete entertainment system, each room designated for sound has its own self-contained system in no way connected to the system of any other room. The fundamentals of the system are determined by the occupant and/or function of the space itself; such systems offer greater individual choice and user flexibility. In this New York apartment, The Audio Consultant designed and installed independent systems in both the master bedroom (left) and living room (right). Interior design by Dexter Design.

cation; and an inefficient use of space.

A **centralized system** allows for total media integration, in which one set of signal/program sources will allocate sight and sound to many rooms by way of remote terminals. Speakers and monitors, however, must be located in those rooms designated for audio-video entertainment. A control panel for remote operation is also necessary. Advantages include maximum flexibility by way of multisource playback and ease of operation. The system is easier and more cost effective to upgrade since there is no duplication of signal/program sources, and it is more space effective.

■ VIDEO COMPONENTS

The video projection system should be one of the first considerations in assembling an integrated entertainment system. Establishing a proper relationship between room dimensions and the projected image is the critical factor besides lighting. The ceiling, which affects the screen size, should be adequately high to accommodate the screen at its proper viewing height—usually designed for an eye level of about four feet from the ground. The volume of the space and its seating arrangement need also be considered. Colorful images in a projection system are visible at about sixty degrees to the left and right of screen center, although it can be up to seventy degrees depending on the particular system. Images are best seen head-on or within thirty degrees from each side of center. The clarity and color saturation of a standard glass-enclosed set is largely unaffected by viewing angle.

The length of the viewing room should be designated in accordance to the distance from the image on the screen to the farthest viewer. A rule of thumb suggests that the distance be less than 6x where x is the width of a single image on the screen. As a final generalization, rear projection units are more space-effective in small areas, while front projection units are more suited to large spaces and permit a greater viewing angle.

■ AUDIO COMPONENTS

As mentioned earlier, the critical listener makes aesthetic concessions in favor of acoustic values. An ideal system includes planar or electrostatic speakers; the speakers themselves are given prime consideration, because they are the component with the most personality. The amplifier is then chosen in light of the listener's special power demands. The turntable choice is more straightforward: The turntable should be of the highest quality, featuring high-resistance to both airborne and structural acoustic feedback, a friction-free assembly structure, and rigid housing. The critical listener's cassette deck, if there is one, is bought on the basis of pure performance rather than on convenience features, in that the critical listener will be willing to forego convenience to accom-

MEDIA | DESIGN

A centralized media unit features one integrated system that drives sound throughout a number of desired spaces. Created by Art Powers, Designed Sound, this system is capable of providing audio in sixteen different rooms. Interior Design by Robert Metzger.

Large projection screens are best mounted at eye level against a black background for maximum visibility and contrast. Lighting should be indirect and rheostat-controlled for glare-free viewing. Interior design by Juan Montoya.

plish good sound. Of greatest importance are a quiet signal-to-noise ratio, low distortion, and a flat frequency response (to provide the deepest bass and the highest highs) as well as AM suppression.

The background listener's requirements determine a rather different set of parameters for component selection. Aesthetics, ease of operation, and convenience are likely to figure prominently in this listener's priorities. The power requirements in this case are generally less than those of the critical enthusiast, with an amplifier requiring somewhere between twenty-five and fifty watts per channel depending on room size and speaker system chosen. Speakers are more likely to be electrodynamic, capable of sounding full at lower volumes. The turntable, probably semi or fully automatic, offers convenience and good quality rather than specific technical features. The tuner probably includes a preset station feature, high selectivity (for drift-free reception), and good multipath rejection. This last element is especially useful in an urban location where signal multiplication often results in a smear and distortion in sound. Finally, an auto-reversing cassette deck and automatic cassette deck changer offers maximum convenience, in that it requires less handling.

Speaker Design

Whatever requirements must be fulfilled, speakers are usually judged by the same criteria that apply to other such devices: uniform frequency response, adequate power-handling ability, and all the other acoustic qualifications that pertain to the sonic accuracy of loudspeaker reproduction. The various types of speakers should be evaluated in terms of the listener's acoustic and aesthetic needs, remembering that the critical listener will more easily make aesthetic compromises in favor of acoustic integrity.

The **electrostatic speaker** was conceived on paper over a century ago and manufactured commercially nearly fifty years ago. At first unreliable, they disappeared from view during the 1930s to be replaced by the rapidly improving electrodynamic speakers. Modern plastics technology in the 1950s and the work of Peter Walker and Arthur Jantzen helped revive their usage and establish their growing popularity.

In principle, the electrostatic speaker features a very thin plastic membrane (diaphragm) suspended between two electromagnets. A high-voltage direct-current charge is maintained between the magnets and the diaphragm. Modulating an electrostatic force on the charged membrane causes it to vibrate and produce sound.

There are advantages to the electrostatic speaker. First, the mass of the membrane is low, yielding a superb transient response (this refers to the speakers' speed in responding to an input signal). More important, coloration, is extremely low, due to the fact that the full control of the diaphragm motion is not dependent on the stiffness or rigidity of the cone. Instead, the electrostatic drive force is exerted uniformly over the entire area of the membrane. The final advantage is that the sound is usually clear and well delineated.

The electrostatic design has limitations as well. Large physical size, somewhat less than perfect bass response, and an amplifier-sensitive quality are the major limitations of the speaker. For reasonably good efficiency the membrane-to-magnet separation must be kept small, but this limits the area available for membrane movement. In order to achieve reasonably high loudness levels the electrostatic speaker must be made physically large, as the volume obtained from any speaker is a function of both the motion of the diaphragm and its area. This limited membrane excursion also serves to curtail the bass output of the speaker, which is further inhibited by the cancellation of the front and rear sound waves produced by the vibrating diaphragm. Also, the electromechanics of the design presents an unusual load impedance to the amplifier, very different from the essentially resistive load that most amplifiers are designed to drive. Results may range from reduced effective power output to increased distortion to outright amplifier failure. The amplifier must be chosen with proper consideration for its intended application. Lastly, positioning is absolutely critical with the electrostatic design. Ideal placement is elevated and as far away from all room boundaries as possible.

A speaker with many of the advantages of the electrostatic but without some of its practical problems is the **planar speaker.** It combines the geometry of the electrostatic with the electrical behavior of the standard dynamic speaker. Like the electrostatic speaker, it features bipolar radiators, features a thin membrane, and has narrow dispersion. The membrane is low in mass, does not have to be stiff or rigid, and is subject to a uniform driving force all over its area. Like the electrostatic design, the membrane is suspended parallel to a metal screen or perforated metal plate. A uniform magnetic force field is established either by making the plates magnetic or by mounting bar magnets on the plates with an electrically conducive grid attached directly to the membrane. When the audio current from the amplifier flows through the wires of the membrane, the fixed and varying magnetic fields create a push-and-pull force and the membrane vibrates. With advantages similar to those of the electrostatic speaker, the planar speaker features the same transient response and freedom from coloration, without requiring the high-voltage supply and without presenting the hard-to-drive complex load to the amplifier that electrostatics do. Size and critical placement are the most obvious disadvantages here.

Dynamic speakers represent the greatest percentage of the current speaker market. Easily the most common type, dynamic speakers feature electrodynamic drivers in the shape of cones or domes enclosed in a box. They are unidirectional but can be adjusted for bipolar sound with multidrivers out the back. Dynamic speakers enjoy such popularity because of a long list of conveniences, the very least of which is cost. They remain durable speakers given to a wide frequency range and good dynamic range. They also feature good dispersion, they present no amplifier problems, and positioning is much more flexible. This is the system for the person who wishes to deal with aesthetics as well as sound. Bipolar radiators—speakers that project sound in two directions—are much more limiting in the design solutions available to them. There seem to be no generic disadvantages—only variable quality depending on the manufacturer.

Competent speaker design—whatever the technical persuasion—has all the different kinds sounding more and more alike. The differences that do exist are trade-offs in such things as acoustic power response, efficiency, and the like. From the listener's point of view the fact that better speakers are sounding more and more alike is worthy of celebration. This means that they are all getting closer to the accurate reproduction of the recorded reality, even though they are approaching the task from different directions.

■AMPLIFICATION AND TONE CONTROLS

Proper amplification is crucial for optimum equipment performance. The heart of the high-fidelity system is, therefore, the amplifier. It is fundamentally a chain of electronic components arranged in such a way that a weak program signal coupled to the input appears at the output in greatly amplified form. Most important, the signal must be capable of adequately driving the loudspeaker, which contributes to the output load.

To maximize a room's listening potential, the best solution is to use an amplifier with enough power—and also speakers with enough power-handling capacity—to

---

LISTENER FATIGUE

Listener fatigue is a function of certain forms of distortion produced by an audio system and is functionally the result of improper speaker placement. The listener may actually become tired after listening to the system for an unduly short period of time; he may even get headaches. Speakers are the most serious potential offenders of this component-dependent problem, because they are the most variable element in the audio chain and are capable of the highest levels of distortion (anywhere from 5% to 20%). Listener fatigue can also be a function of the sound-pressure level, a measure of the volume in decibels; an overly "bright" room with too many reflective surfaces will be too reverberant.

Amplifier/speaker imbalance can also cause this condition. If an amplifier is under-powered (trying to produce a signal greater than its capacity), for example, clipping will result. This can be audible as a harsh, highly irritable form of metallic distortion. You can avoid potential listener fatigue listening to and comparing many speakers before you make your final purchase.

produce adequate listening levels without much reflective reinforcement from the room. This should yield the cleanest sound a system can produce. Strictly speaking, amplifier power is a function of room size, reverberation time, and speaker efficiency—and the volume at which one generally listens to the system. The power will need to be stepped up proportionally with less efficient speakers and for larger rooms. It follows that the more absorbent a room, the greater the amplifier power required for a given sound intensity. The ambient noise level of the room also affects the power requirement, since the transmitted sounds have to outweigh the ambient noise.

Correct and judicious use of the controls on audio components is essential to maximizing a system's performance in a given space. Acoustic shortcomings in the listening room, the program signal, or the speakers may sometimes make it necessary to boost the treble or bass frequencies to such an extent that a flat frequency sound results. This is called equalizing, and it is performed on the signal as it passes through the amplifier. The bass and treble tone controls of the amplifier are the most simple controls available.

All the frequencies of the audible spectrum should ideally enjoy equal amplification from the microphone to the loudspeaker. Although equal amplification at all frequencies is one of the aims of high fidelity, its accurate maintenance is nearly impossible without some means of easy correction. The inherent potential for one selected frequency to receive more or less amplification than another is limitless. Correcting the frequency/amplitude characteristics of the signal is one of the functions of the tone controls. The controls correct not only signal shortcomings but acoustic shortcomings in the room as well.

The possibility of frequency/amplitude error lies in both the recording of the program software itself and in the program sources themselves. Irregularities in the processing, for example, may cause a loss in treble or a weak bass register. Deficiencies of this nature can be corrected by applying an appropriate treble or bass boost by way of the tone controls. Some of the smaller loudspeakers will yield a better bass performance if the low-frequency energy signal fed to them is slightly augmented—by way of the tone controls. Extreme care must be exercised in these cases, as it is easy to overload small speakers with too much bass, thereby precipitating low-frequency distortion. Small speakers cannot be expected to yield the bass performance of their larger more costly counterparts.

The tone controls can also be used to correct for peaks in the overall response characteristic. A mild reduction of the treble control might tame a treble (or high-frequency) peak, ridding the reproduction of overbrightness. A peak of this kind can be detected as a squeaky background noise. Similarly, low-frequency peaks arising from room or loudspeaker resonance can partly be corrected by appropriately cutting the bass.

Although tone controls can be employed to help correct a particular deficiency, it is clear that for optimum correction a graphic equalizer is required. The simplest form of equalizer found in professional use is the simple bass and treble control.

> **PROJECTION GUIDELINES**
>
> The projection system's requirements will closely affect the spatial, lighting, and seating arrangements.
>
> Establishing a proper relationship between the projected image and the room dimensions should be one of the first priorities. The length of the room should be determined according to the distance from the image on the screen to the farthest viewer. Seating arrangement would then be image dependent. A rule of thumb is that the distance be less than 6(x) where (x) is the width of a single image on the screen. This condition is easily accommodated with a front projection system.
>
> Rear projection units are recommended in smaller spaces that might encounter variable lighting levels. The disadvantage, however, is that rear projection units reduce the viewing angles and seating area. This would of course curtail the use of a more expanded seating arrangement and therefore the number of people who can view the screen as well. Furthermore when rear projection is chosen, the 6(x) distance becomes impractical since the space behind the screen is limited in size. To compensate for minimal space, focal-length lenses are used in rear projection to shorten the distance, which also reduces the viewing area in front of the screen. However, a case for rear projection can be made in that it can be seen in normal lighting levels without sacrificing clarity. Front projection is possible in brighter light using projectors with high output lamps rather than conventional models that require a darker room.

Other Details

■ **WIRING AND PHASING**

The wiring and connection process of an entertainment system is admittedly complicated. An effective and intelligent wiring plan will allow component interphase to yield the greatest amount of convenience and satisfaction.

An electrical analysis of the residence and the listening/viewing room should be conducted in relation to the equipment selected and the relative electrical demands of each. This should most logically be done at the earliest stages of the construction or design process so that adjustments can be made with the least amount of disturbance. Single-family houses provide the greatest room for expansion, while urban apartments are more limiting. In the latter case, you are generally restricted to whatever current capabilities are already supplied, although you may be permitted to run a main feed from the basement into the apartment.

In a best-case situation, a separate feed runs straight from the main junction box to the individual components. This would not only improve the reliability and performance but it would isolate it from other household electrical problems, facilitating any maintenance or service that may be required.

There must also be an ample number of wall outlets behind any proposed wall units so as not to overload any one outlet. Two

TESTING AND DEBUGGING

A system must be tested as a final step to component installation. This is best done after approximately one week, during which time you have familiarized yourself with the operation and capabilities of the system. This is also the time to consider unanticipated needs and changes of heart. Acoustic integrity is judged at this time. In sum, deductive reasoning indicates that there is a greater chance of component failure in a sophisticated, complex system than there is in a more simple system. Still, actual debugging is necessary only if a malfunction does exist. More often than not, the malfunction is in the wiring. Backtrack your wiring connections to see if this is indeed the case. If the problem lies elsewhere, you will have to contact a specialist or reexamine the entire system.

For Club Med's New York headquarters, architect Karl Christopher designed all the company's public and private spaces including a second-floor screening room. In addition to the overhead lighting, Christopher specified an edge-lit niche to run along the room's perimeter walls; because of its soft light, the latter is often used as the sole source of illumination during a screening.

fourplex boxes (8 inputs) mounted on the rear wall midway between the highest and lowest components should provide the correct amount of power and convenience. Should additional connections become necessary after construction has been completed, use an industrial heavy-duty terminal outlet strip connected to a wall outlet. One option to consider is the installation and use of a wall-mounted switch, to control all the components together rather than separately.

When conducting an electrical analysis, besides determining what is currently available, you should determine *anticipated* needs. First, consider the electrical draw of each component when in use (continuous current carrying capacity). More important, however, is the inrush current, which is determined by a formula: The amperage draw when an electrical device is turned on should be 6(x) that of its continuous current carrying capacity (cccc). Both the cccc and the amperage draw are provided in the manufacturer's specifications. Based on this somewhat loose set of parameters, a general measure for an integrated audio-video system of moderate sophistication runs at 20 amps.

Rules governing component connections and wiring are straightforward and simple:

1. Use good quality low-loss cable and firm clean contacts.
2. Hide speaker wires under carpeting (preferably avoiding the more heavily trafficked routes), through walls, or behind floorboards.
3. Select a cable no thinner than a 16-gage multistrand copper wire (lamp cord). A considerably thicker speaker wire (Monster Cable) is available and recommended for highest-quality performance. Technically, the Monster Cable delivers all the power the amp has to put out with no line loss (loss of the signal through the wire).

For video connections a good quality low-loss cable with a high radio-frequency shielding value is desirable. In a multi strand wire the center wire is the control power carrier while the outer wire shields it from picking up other signals.

Electrical phasing is a function of continuous polarities. Both the amplifier and the speakers contain positive and negative connectors. To make it easier for consumers and to facilitate proper phasing, left and right loudspeaker terminals on both the amplifier and the speakers themselves are color-coded. Confused stereo images result from incorrect phasing. Bass reproduction is also inhibited.

■ LIGHTING

Lighting is a crucial factor in the design of a media space and should be evaluated in terms of video projection guidelines. It has a direct effect on the receipt and perception of video images and therefore determines the performance of the electronics as well as the comfort of the room. In general, a level of brightness capable of transmitting a clear, sharp image without overpowering the atmosphere must be maintained. An intelligent lighting plan adjusted to the room's media requirements is best made during the initial stages of design. This affords the greatest degree of control and flexibility. Installing video in an already illuminated space presents its own special problems and solutions. If you are adding components to an area that is already in use you will probably want to replace fixtures or lamps and add any accessories necessary to achieve the desired effect or control. Evaluate natural light as well as artificial light in terms of control, source, and direction. Flourescent lighting is generally discouraged as it can interfere with viewing images on the CRT screen.

As a starting point, most experts agree that projection televisions function optimally in a totally darkened space. Daylight viewing can yield halated images and a noticeable loss of luminosity. A worst-case situation has light entering the room from behind the screen, while a best-case situation has the light originating from behind the viewer. Control of the daylight is a function of the window treatment (shades, blinds, drapes, opaque screens) and location of the screen itself, which in turn, is technology dependent. State-of-the-art two-piece front-projection units offer the most limitations; the one-piece front-projection unit the least, with the rear-projection units somewhere in between. In the same context, high-resolution monitors and monitor/receivers usually will pose fewer limitations than those encountered in conventional television sets.

The principles in lighting seem simple enough. Nothing much has changed since good viewing habits were being promulgated in the 1950s. They are:
1. never watch anything in a totally darkened space
2. never allow anything to shine onto the screen
3. never allow anything to obstruct a view of the screen
4. place a light source behind the viewer's head.

Diffused light originating from behind the viewer will not reflect onto the screen from a reasonable distance. The light's origin should be indirect, balanced, rheostat-controlled and multicircuited. Multicircuit lighting allows for different sets of lights in the same room to be separately controlled by its own switch or rheostat.

ROOM COLOR
Room color is also a consideration to be evaluated in putting a system together. A darker colored room with nonreflective surfaces usually offers the best environment for viewing, with minimal reflectivity and the greatest degree of contrast. Primary colors in the pure sense should be avoided as they will tend to contaminate the integrity of the projected images on the screen.

Creative use of lighting must therefore be considered in terms of video usage, equipment, and user expectations. In such situations it is the screen rather than the projector that must be taken into consideration. The component reflects; it does not discern. Judicious placement of light fixtures is therefore critical. As a rule, the light source should not fall on the screen itself, so recessed highhats are preferable to surface-mounted fixtures. Wall washes, uplights, cove lighting (an indirect lighting technique where the lamps are located along the ceiling perimeter line and concealed with a baffle or molding), and wall sconces are also conditionally recommended. Proper intensity adjustment (in the case of a rheostat), modulated wattage, and sensible balance so that the light is not all originating from the same source must also be examined. Surface-mounted fixtures allow the option of rheostat control and multicircuit wiring but are somewhat more obtrusive. Certain fixture accessories such as barn doors, louvers, and antidazzling grilles are helpful in deflecting the lamp's beam.

Audio task-lighting must also be considered; this is best planned in conjunction with any cabinetry you are adding. New developments have produced specially designed fixtures to aid the operation of audio equipment in low ambient light. More often found in clubs or discos, fixtures of this kind are working their way into the home because they are small, focused, and well designed. Created to mount directly on the equipment, adjacent wall, adjacent cabinet, or turntable dust cover, these lights provide glarefree illumination for cueing or equipment maintenance.

Some feature a rotating shield that permits the adjustment of light intensity and coverage. When the lights are mounted on a dust cover, a switch automatically turns the light on when the cover is lifted and turns it off when the lid is closed.

Additional alternatives for task lighting include automatic on-off lighting on the hinges of the media cabinet doors: Opening the doors activates the lights, allowing easy visual access to the controls even when the room lights are low. Another option, tube lights—strips of narrow incandescent lighting—are best used when attached to the underside of a shelf just behind the fascia or along the inside perimeter of the cabinet.

The Future

The future of the audio/video domain is as limitless as the imagination. In audio it is to achieve the highest fidelity; in video, the superlative image. Both are undoubtedly an endless life's work. There are, however, some more tangible expectations to discuss, especially in light of recent technological developments.

Voice-activated audio-video systems will no doubt become the rule. They are, in fact, in prototype form now. This type of system will respond to prerecorded verbal commands, making the wireless remote virtually obsolete. This calls for more interface between the listener and the system, yet makes listening easier.

Personal record, tape, and disc libraries will probably become obsolete in favor of a central library network. Here the listener will actually be interfacing with a library in which digitally reproduced signals can literally retrieve any selection desired that the library has.

Prototypes of digital recorders are currently emerging. Eliminating all moving parts, an electronic sensor will scan, read, and play musical recordings stored on what looks like a credit card. Advances in the computer microprocessor, large-scale integrated circuit, and very large-scale integrated circuit have made this innovation possible.

In video the perfectly flat screen—displaying a picture free of distortion and jitter—and three-dimensional viewing are already on the horizon. It seems that at almost any moment, high-resolution screens with pictures created by 1125 lines of resolution (instead of 525) together with "touch sensitive" screens, will be a practical reality. Data networks are already becoming a vast new industry as information service becomes the pay television of the 80s. A new form of video information—**videotext**—employs still pictures, printed words, numbers, and even photographs to create a new hybrid information network. The result will be a kind of newspaper/encyclopedia/almanac combined with service data such as airline reservations, stock quotes, and the like.

Audiotext will permit data retrieval by telephone rather than by computer. Responses will be transmitted in answer to requests made by punching the buttons on a touch-tone-telephone keypad. Most of the systems work by recording speech and converting it into a digital code that can be stored on a computer. The computer simply strings the appropriate phrases together depending on the request.

The turntable will become outdated the soonest of all our currently family componentry, and the LP record's days are numbered. The compact disc has demonstrated itself to be superior in all respects: wider band width, better frequency response, better signal-to-noise ratio, better dynamic range, and easier-to-operate and more durable software. It is simply an effective replacement.

The future should continue to provide improvements in software, with a wider variety of titles available as well as an increased library of the old material.

Tuners will become more efficient with stereo, digitized, AM broadcasts that will virtually eliminate all background noise. Technology will see a constantly improving signal-to-noise ratio and improved capture ratio (ability to grab a station and hold it). More user-friendly machines are expected

FROM THE OFFICE TO THE HOME

Historically office design has been a facilities function concerned with housing people and their equipment in a setting laid out to promote efficiency. In most cases the equipment consisted of telephones, typewriters, desk calculators, and the like. And the design strategy—if indeed there was one—was concerned with simply accommodating the devices on their work surfaces. Those larger, more complex pieces of equipment were installed in separate data centers safely away from the workspace proper.

However, the current trend in the office technology field is to move machine capabilities out of the technology centers and into the office workspace. In the office, machines are no longer devices exclusively used to mechanize and process repetitive tasks (such routine tasks as managing payroll and checking inventories have long since been turned over to computers). Rather, they have become tools to expand one's intellectual capabilities. The video display terminal and similar devices will soon be as commonplace and essential as the telephone.

Integration into the home, however, has been noticeably slower. Inhibited by expensive equipment, a continually changing technology and user skepticism and resistance have all contributed to the process. Closer examination, however, will reveal that many of these concerns are quickly disappearing. On the positive side, two developments that should help domestic integration are component video and the new software.

in which the circuitry will automatically optimize itself depending on the conditions.

Traditionally the least efficient component, the amplifier will most likely diminish this current reputation. Greater use of the vacuum tube will provide amplifiers with greater linear transferring characteristics than the bipolar transistor.

One might predict that the reel-to-reel tape deck is on its way out because of its large and cumbersome format. Cassette decks will continue to use digital technology, realizing benefits of the disc player with the convenience of the cassette.

Beta and VHS high-fidelity represent the first truly high-quality integration of audio and video to date, storing the audio and video on tape operating at fifteen inches per second. Magnetic tape remains our only recording medium.

Technology should move toward the integration of the preamplifier/control center so that there is one master panel. There will be such controls as image enhancers and detailers, in effect, the equivalent of audio tone controls.

There is really no new speaker technology of equal magnitude to digital audio, although there will continue to be an increased use of manmade material in speaker fabrication. Microspeakers will, however, be improved to project a wider range of sound. Because of the new demands posed by the digital age, speakers will soon be capable of wider band width, increased dynamic range, and faster transient response. Use of horn drivers will continue to decrease, and the shape of the cones themselves should go from circular to square shape.

The future of sound processors such as equalizers, noise-reduction units, and compressor/expander units is somewhat doubtful. Electronics will eventually automatically analyze and correct deficiencies in the speaker/listening room interface, thereby eliminating the need for signal processors. For the time being, they will continue to become more user-friendly and more available to a wider audience of consumers and provide complete room equalizations.

The current proliferation of electronic media equipment continues to saturate an already overcrowded marketplace. No sooner is a component introduced than it is outmoded by a more compact and more user-friendly version, which only intensifies the challenge of assembling an effective entertainment system. For this reason, today's equipment occupies a position of far greater importance than it did five years ago. Awareness and education are the foundation of an intelligent planner. It is only by understanding each individual component—its functions, capabilities, and requirements—that listener/viewer satisfaction and maximum performance will be attained.

Glossary

AC—Alternating current; the kind of electrical power available from wall outlets in the United States and Canada. AC is rated at 110 to 120 volts.

Acoustic Center—The point at which a sound wave appears to originate in a loudspeaker.

Acoustic Feedback—Loudspeaker vibrations picked up by a turntable. If these vibrations reach the cartridge, noise (a howl or a rumble) and/or distortion occurs.

AFC—Automatic frequency control, sometimes called automatic fine tuning in color television; locks the FM or TV receiver to a station frequency.

Alignment—An adjustment that brings a component into conformance with published specifications.

AM Suppression—The ability of an FM tuner to reject AM signals.

Ambience—The acoustical atmosphere that results from multiple echoes within the listening enclosure. It is responsible for the coloration of the concert hall, auditorium, listening room, etc.

Amplifier—The electronic component that supplies power to a loudspeaker system(s) and is designed to pick up weak signals from other components. An integrated amplifier incorporates a preamplifier, which provides appropriate equalization and control for various program sources such as a turntable, tuner, or tape. (See also **Preamplifier**.)

Anechoic Chamber—A reflection-free environment generally used for the testing of microphones, loudspeakers, and other devices.

Antenna—A device that intercepts radio waves and converts them into electrical signals suitable for a receiver or tuner.

Audio Spectrum—The full range of audio frequencies, from the lowest to the highest (15 Hz to 20,000 Hz).

AVC—Automatic volume control; maintains a constant sound level despite differences in the strength of an incoming signal.

Balance—The relative levels of two or more signal paths, recorded tracks, or instruments.

Bandwidth—The range between the upper and lower cut-off frequencies of an audio system.

Bass—The lowest portion of the perceived audio spectrum.

Belt Drive—A turntable with a platter that is rotated by a belt attached to a motor pulley.

Bidirectional—The ability of an open reel or cassette recorder to play (and in some cases record) both stereo track pairs on a tape by simply reversing the tape's direction; there is no need to remove and replace the reels or cassettes for the process.

Cartridge—The device that holds the stylus and translates its motion in the record groove into an electrical signal.

Cassette—A compact, enclosed type of tape cartridge containing two reels.

CATV—Community antenna television, or cable television.

CED—Capacitance electronic disc; a system of video recording on a grooved disc.

Coloration—A deviation in the balance of musical sounds usually audible as heavy bass, prominent mid-range, or exaggerated high-frequency reproduction.

Compact Stereo—A stereophonic sound system consisting of three or more separate pieces that is usually sold as a single package.

Component Stereo—A stereophonic sound system made up of separate components (tuner, turntable, amplifier, etc.) individually selected by the purchaser.

Crossover Network—A filter that splits a frequency response into two or more paths; low frequencies are passed to a woofer, middle frequencies to a mid-range driver, and high frequencies to a tweeter.

Cueing Device—A control with which one can raise and lower the tonearm without directly handling it.

Damper—A device that progressively weakens the electrical or acoustical energy or signal in a given space. Acoustical panels or sound-absorbing decor are examples.

Decay Time—The time it takes for echoes and reverberation to die away.

Decibel—The relative intensity of a sound or the relative strength of a signal expressed as a logarithmic expression of acoustical or electrical ratios.

Direct Drive—A turntable with a platter that rests directly on the motor shaft; no intermediate coupling devices are used.

Direct Sound—A sound without echoes or reverberation; one that reaches the listener via a straight path from the sound source.

Distortion—Any alteration (excluding amplitude) between the input and output of an electronic or acoustical device. Distortion is measured as a percentage of the total waveform amplitude.

Dolby—A system of noise/hiss reduction invented by Ray Dolby.

Drift—An extended deviation from a specified tape speed in a tape recorder.

Driver—Any individual speaker within a system, such as the woofer or tweeter.

Dynamic Range—The range of amplitudes in music from the loudest passages to the softest passages; generally expressed in decibels.

Electrostatic—A drive system for speakers employing a thin plastic membrane or diaphragm suspended in an electrostatic field. Changes in the signal voltage move the diaphragm, creating a sound pressure wave.

Equalization—As a function of speaker/room interface, equalization involves the manipulation of a frequency response to produce a desired effect.

Equalizer—A signal processing device used to change the frequency response of the signal passing through it; a graphic equalizer features slide controls that give a graphic representation of their frequency response characteristics.

Expander—A device used to restore natural dynamic range in the making of recordings and in broadcasting.

Feedback—The return of some portion of an output signal to the system's input, which is then reamplified and added to the new input. Acoustic feedback is discerned as an audible howl or squeal.

Filter—An equalizer designed to weaken certain frequencies or bands of frequencies.

Flutter—Variations in the speed of a turntable or tape that results in a muddy sound quality.

Frequency—The number of vibrations per unit of time. Measured in hertz.

GLOSSARY

Frequency Range—The range of frequencies over which an audio component will operate.

Generation—A copy of a tape; the original recording is the first generation tape, a copy of the original is a second generation, etc.

Hardware—The general term applied to all audio, video, and computer equipment.

Head—The device in a tape recorder that physically contacts the tape to read the magnetic impulses.

High-Output Tape—High-sensitivity tape.

Hue—A control that modifies the color values in a television picture.

Hum—A low-frequency noise generally caused by an incomplete ground of the power line.

Image Shift—A change in the apparent location of a recorded sound source.

Infrared Remote Control—A generally hand-held device that permits the controlling of certain equipment without wires or cables. It utilizes infrared radiation to transmit control information.

Integrated Amplifier—A single component that combines the functions and circuitry of a power amplifier and a preamplifier.

Interface—The proper interconnection of two components or systems.

Lead-In—A wire or cable connecting an antenna to a television.

LED—Light-emitting diode; an indicator often used in read-out displays that gives off light when an electric current is passed through it. It is commonly used in volume level and tuning.

Linear Tracking—Refers to the straight-line movement of a tonearm.

Loudness—The intensity of a sound based on a subjective impression.

Loudspeaker—A transducer that converts electrical energy into acoustical energy.

Microcomponents—Miniaturized audio components that offer the benefits of traditional-sized components in far less space.

Midrange—A loudspeaker specifically designed to reproduce frequencies from 500Hz to 2500Hz.

Modem—A device used to connect a computer to a telephone.

Monitor—A television set or computer screen system, with or without an audio system.

Noise—An extraneous sound or signal added to an original recording. In audio, noise is generally heard as a hiss or hum.

Noise, Ambient—Noise in the environment, in the absence of extraneous sound sources.

Noise Reduction System—A signal processing system designed to weaken noise components in an audio system.

Overload—The distortion that is produced when a signal exceeds the level at which the system will produce its maximum output level.

Pitch Control—A control for increasing or decreasing the speed of a turntable or tape deck.

Polarity—Refers to the positive or negative direction of an electrical or magnetic force.

Power Supply—A circuit supplying direct current power to an amplifier or other electronic system.

Preamplifier—A switching, amplification, and equalization component designed to select input signals, amplify them, and deliver an output voltage to a power amplifier.

Resonance—The naturally occurring frequency at which an object (e.g. wall, air, loudspeaker) may be excited into motion. In loudspeakers unwanted resonances cause colorations in sound quality. Room resonance is a function of the dimensions of a room.

Reverberation—The perceived continuation of a sound resulting from its reflection off of exposed surfaces in a room.

RF—Radio frequency; the full range of frequencies pertaining to and associated with radiant energy, specifically those frequencies employed in radio and television.

Selectivity—The ability of a tuner to receive the desired station while rejecting adjacent stations.

Sensitivity—The input signal level required by a tuner, amplifier, etc. to produce a stated output. The lower the input necessary, the higher the sensitivity.

Separation—The extent to which two stereo channels are kept apart. The larger the number (expressed in decibels), the better the separation.

Signal—An electrical replica of an actual sound.

Signal Processing Device—A component (such as an equalizer, compressor, or expander) used to modify a signal passing through it.

Signal-to-Noise Ratio—The proportion of signal to extraneous noise in a high-fidelity system. The higher the S/N ratio, the better the system.

SPL—Sound pressure level; the loudness level of a speaker relative to a specified input signal. It is usually stated in decibels.

Stylus—The specially shaped tip that rides in a record groove. The cartridge and stylus are held by the tonearm.

Synthesizer—A system that generates a precise and stable frequency.

Tone Control—Controls for modifying the level of bass, treble, or midrange frequencies.

Tonearm—The part of a record player that supports the cartridge.

Tracking—The ability of a phonograph pickup to properly follow a record groove.

Transducer—Any device (such as a tape head or speaker) that converts one type of energy (electrical, acoustical, magnetic, electrical) into another. A loudspeaker is an electro-acoustical transducer.

Tuner—The portion of a radio or television set that selects the desired incoming signal.

Turntable—A record-playing device consisting of a motor-driven platter, a tonearm to which the phono cartridge is attached, and a base on which the entire assembly is mounted.

Tweeter—High frequency (treble) loudspeaker.

Videocassette—A videotape packaged in a cassette or cartridge format.

Videodisc—A flat disc designed to play prerecorded visual information. It is accepted by a player attached to a standard television receiver.

Woofer—Low frequency (bass) loudspeaker.

Wow—Distortion resulting from irregularities in the speed at which a record or tape recording is played.

Useful Addresses

ARCHITECTS AND DESIGNERS

ANTINE/POLO, LIMITED
276 Lydecker Street
Englewood, NJ 07631
(201) 568–4862
(212) 690–0094

ERIC BERNARD DESIGNS
177 East 94th Street
New York, NY 10128
(212) 876–9295

BRAY-SCHAIBLE DESIGNS
INCORPORATED
80 West 40th Street
New York, NY 10018
(212) 354–7525

BROMLEY/JACOBSEN
242 West 27th Street
New York, NY 10001
(212) 620–4250

NICHOLAS A. CALDER INTERIORS
348 East 58th Street
New York, NY 10022
(212) 308–6670

DEXTER DESIGN INCORPORATED
Interior Design
133 East 58th Street
New York, NY 10022
(212) 752–2426

ANGELO DONGHIA
Donghia Associates, Incorporated,
Residential Division
315 East 62nd Street
New York, NY 10021
(212) 838–9100

FALKENER-STUETLEY INTERIORS,
LIMITED
50 Pierrepont Street
Brooklyn Heights, NY 11201
(212) 624–4718

STANLEY JAY FRIEDMAN,
INCORPORATED
200 East 71st Street
New York, NY 10021
(212) 988–3595

GENSLER & ASSOCIATES
823 United Nations Plaza
Suite 500
New York, NY 10017
(212) 286–0212

CAROLYN GUTTILLA/PLAZA ONE
8 Birch Hill Road
Locust Valley, NY 11560
(516) 671–9280

GWATHMEY SIEGEL & ASSOCIATES
ARCHITECTS
475 Tenth Avenue
New York, NY 10018
(212) 947–1240

INTRADESIGN, INCORPORATED
717 La Cienega Boulevard
Los Angeles, CA 90069
(213) 652–6114

NOEL JEFFREY INCORPORATED
Interior Design
22 East 65th Street
New York, NY 10021
(212) 535–0300

FRANCISCO KRIPACZ
125 North Robertson Boulevard
Los Angeles, CA 90048
(213) 278–1915

GERALD KUHN, INCORPORATED
88 Lexington Avenue
New York, NY 10016
(212) 889–6584

RICHARD D. LAWRENCE ASSOCIATES
25 Sutton Place North
New York, NY 10022
(212) 752–2930

MARIO LOCICERO, INCORPORATED
343 West 71st Street
New York, NY 10023
(212) 873–2439

SAM LOPATA, INCORPORATED
27 West 20th Street
New York, NY 10011
(212) 691–7924

STEPHEN MALLORY ASSOCIATES
INCORPORATED
170 East 61st Street
New York, NY 10021
(212) 826–6350

ROBERT METZGER INTERIORS
210 East 58th Street
New York, NY 10022
(212) 371–9800

JUAN MONTOYA DESIGN
CORPORATION
80 Eighth Avenue
New York, NY 10011
(212) 242–3622

PATINO/WOLF ASSOCIATES
INCORPORATED
400 East 52nd Street
New York, NY 10022
(212) 355–6581

RUBÉN DE SAAVEDRA, ASID
225 East 57th Street
New York, NY 10022
(212) 759–2892

MICHAEL DE SANTIS, INCORPORATED
Interiors, ASID
1110 Second Avenue
New York, NY 10022
(212) 753–8871

SCRUGGS•MYERS & ASSOCIATES
25 West 15th Street
New York, NY 10011
(212) 255–2066

DAVID SNYDER
Vice President Fashion
Marshall Fields
111 North State Street
Chicago, IL 60690
(312) 781–5741

KATHERINE STEPHENS ASSOCIATES
INCORPORATED
6 Dianas Circle
Roslyn Estates, NY 11576
(516) 621–1460
(212) 764–1711

MICHAEL TAYLOR INTERIOR DESIGN
No. 9 25th Avenue North
San Francisco, CA 94121
(415) 668–7668

ADAM D. TIHANY INTERNATIONAL
LIMITED
57 East 11th Street
New York, NY 10003
(212) 505–2360

CALVIN TSAO & ZACK MCKOWN
146 Central Park West
New York, NY 10023
(212) 496–0320

WALZ DESIGN INC
141 Fifth Avenue
New York, NY 10010
(212) 477–2211

PHOTOGRAPHERS

JAIME ARDILES-ARCE
663 Fifth Avenue
New York, NY 10022
(212) 371–4749

HEDRICH BLESSING
11 West Illinois Street
Chicago, IL 60610
(312) 321–1151

DAVID BUXBAUM
15 East 30th Street
Suite 2E
New York, NY 10016
(212) 689–5985

DERRICK & LOVE INTERIOR
PHOTOGRAPHY
333 West 19th Street
New York, NY 10011
(212) 243–7339

DANIEL EIFERT
26 Second Avenue
New York, NY 10003
(212) 473–2562

PHILLIP H. ENNIS PHOTOGRAPHY
8 Makamah Beach Road
Northport, NY 11768
(516) 754–2638

MARY HARTY/PETER DE ROSA
171–33 Bagley Avenue
Flushing, NY 11358
(212) 864–3007
(516) 324–0231

NORMAN MCGRATH PHOTOGRAPHY
164 West 79th Street
New York, NY 10024
(212) 799–6422

KEITH SCOTT MORTON
39 West 29th Street
New York, NY 10001
(212) 889–6643

PETER PAIGE PHOTOGRAPHY
37 West Homestead Avenue
Palisades Park, NJ 07650
(201) 592–7889

USEFUL ADDRESSES

MARK ROSS PHOTOGRAPHY, INCORPORATED
345 East 80th Street
New York, NY 10021
(212) 744–7258

BILL ROTHSCHILD ARCHITECTURAL PHOTOGRAPHER
19 Judith Lane
Monsey, NY 10952
(212) 752–3674
(914) 354–4567

KEN SPENCER
c/o Newsday Magazine
235 Pinelawn Road
Melville, NY 11747
(516) 454–2309

PETER VITALE PHOTOGRAPHY
157 East 71st Street
New York, NY 10021
(212) 249–8412

PAUL WARCHOL PHOTOGRAPHY
18 East 16th Street
New York, NY 10003
(212) 929–8770

AUDIO AND VIDEO MANUFACTURERS

ACCULAB BY RTR INDUSTRIES
8116 Deering Avenue
Canoga Park, CA 91304

ACCUPHASE BY D&K IMPORTS
146 East Post Road
White Plains, NY 10601

ACOUSTAT CORPORATION
3101 Southwest First Terrace
Fort Lauderdale, FL 33315

ACOUSTICAL PHYSICS LABS
151 6th Street NW
Atlanta, GA 30313

ACOUSTIC DESIGN GROUP
PO Box G3
Aspen, CO 81612

ACOUSTIC INTERFACE
PO Box 6632
Santa Barbara, CA 93060

ACOUSTIC RESEARCH (TELEDYNE ACOUSTIC RESEARCH)
10 American Drive
Norwood, MA 02062

ACOUSTI-PHASE
PO Box 207
Proctorsville, VT 05153

ADA (Audio Design Associates)
602–610 Mamaroneck Ave.
White Plains, NY 10605

ADC, AUDIO DYNAMICS CORP.
Division BSR, USA, Ltd.
Pickett District Road
New Milford, CT 06776

ADS (Analog & Digital Systems, Incorporated)
One Progress Way
Wilmington, MA 01887

ADVENT DIVISION INTERNATIONAL JENSEN INCORPORATED, AN ESMARK COMPANY
4136 North United Parkway
Schiller Park, IL 60176

AGI, AUDIO GENERAL INCORPORATED
1631 Easton Road
Willow Grove, PA 19090

AIWA AMERICA INCORPORATED
35 Oxford Drive
Moonachie, NJ 07074

AKAI AMERICA LIMITED
800 West Artesia Boulevard
PO Box 6010
Compton, CA 90220

AKG ACOUSTICS, PHILIPS AUDIO VIDEO SYSTEMS CORPORATION
77 Selleck Street
Stamford, CT 06902

ALARON INCORPORATED
185 Park Street
PO Box 550
Troy, MI 48099

ALLISON ACOUSTICS, INCORPORATED
7 Tech Circle
Natick, MA 01760

ALPINE ELECTRONICS OF AMERICA
3102 Kashiwa Street
Torrance, CA 90505

ALPINE/LUXMAN
19145 Gramercy Place
Torrance, CA 90501

ALTEC LANSING INTERNATIONAL
PO Box 3113
Anaheim, CA 92803

AMBER ELECTRONICS, INCORPORATED
500 Henry Avenue
Charlottesville, VA 22901

AMPEX
401 Broadway
Redwood City, CA 94063

ANDANTE BY SUMIKO
PO Box 5046
Berkeley, CA 94705

ANGLO-AMERICAN AUDIO
PO Box 653
Buffalo, NY 14240

APATURE
Division, ACR Industries
RFD #1, Rt. 2
Preston, CT 06360

API, AUDIO PRODUCTS INTERNATIONAL
161 Don Park Road
Markham, Ontario
Canada L3R 1C2

APOGEE ACOUSTICS
920 Providence Highway
Norwood, MA 02062

ASTATIC CORPORATION
Corner of Harbor & Jackson Streets
Conneaut, OH 44030

AUDIO CONTROL CORPORATION
6520 212th Street SW
Lynnwood, WA 98036

AUDIO DESIGN
PO Box 1250, Fall Station
Niagara Falls, NY 14303

AUDIONICS
PO Box 969, University Station
Portland, OR 97207

AUDIOPHILE PRODUCTS
7800 Airpark Road #17
Gaithersburg, MD 20879

AUDIOPHILE SYSTEMS
6842 Hawthorne Park Drive
Indianapolis, IN 46220

AUDIO PRO, INTERSEARCH INCORPORATED
4720-Q Boston Way
Lanham, MD 20801

AUDIO RESEARCH CORPORATION
6801 Shingle Creek Parkway
Minneapolis, MN 55430

AUDIOSOURCE
1185 Chess Drive
Foster City, CA 94404

AUDIO-TECHNICA U.S., INCORPORATED
1221 Commerce Drive
Stow, OH 44224

AUDIO TECHNOLOGY
1169 Tower Road
Schaumburg, IL 60195

■

BABB CORPORATION
11562 Chairman Drive
Dallas, TX 75243

B&W LOUDSPEAKERS LIMITED, ANGLO-AMERICAN AUDIO
286 Brentwood Drive
Hudson, OH 44236

1200 Markham Road No. 506
Scarborough, Ontario
Canada M1H 3C3

PO Box 653
Buffalo, NY 14240

BANG & OLUFSEN OF AMERICA, INCORPORATED
515 Busse Road
Elk Grove Village, IL 60007

BASF SYSTEMS, BASF WYANDOTTE CORPORATION
10 Crosby Drive
Bedford, MA 01730

BECKER ELECTRONICS
Route 145
East Durham, NY 12423

BEDINI ELECTRONICS
13,000 San Fernando Road, Unit 9
Sylmar, CA 91342

BEL, BROWN ELECTRONIC LABS
1233 Somerset Drive
San Jose, CA 95132

BELL & HOWELL CO. (VIDEO SYSTEMS)
60 East 42nd Street
New York, NY 10165

BENJAMIN ELECTROPRODUCTS, INCORPORATED
75 Austin Boulevard
Commack, NY 11725

B.E.S. (BERTAGNI ELECTROACOUSTIC SYSTEMS, INCORPORATED)
345 Fischer Street
Costa Mesa, CA 92626

HAROLD BEVERIDGE INCORPORATED
505 E. Montecito Street
Santa Barbara, CA 93103

BEYER/DYNAMIC, BURNS AUDIOTRONICS, INCORPORATED
5-05 Burns Avenue
Hicksville, NY 11801

BGW SYSTEMS
13130 South Yukon Avenue
Hawthorne, CA 90250

B&K COMPONENTS
PO BOX 331
Orchard Park, NY 14127

BIAMP SYSTEMS, INCORPORATED
9600 SW Barnes Road
Portland, OR 97225

DESIGN

BLAUPUNKT, ROBERT BOSCH CORPORATION
2400 South 25th Avenue
Broadview, IL 60153

BML ELECTRONICS
5305 North Ravenswood
Chicago, IL 60640

BOOTHROYD STUART/MERIDIAN
1200 Markham Road
Scarborough, Ontario
Canada M1H 3C3

BOSE CORPORATION
The Mountain
Framingham, MA 01701

BOSTON ACOUSTICS
247 Lynnfield Street
Peabody, MA 01960

BOULTON STEREO SYSTEMS
380 Madison Avenue
New York, NY 10016

BOZAK, INCORPORATED
68 Holmes Road
Newington, CT 06111

BRANDENBURG LOUDSPEAKER COMPANY
186 South Main Street
Fall River, MA 02721

BROADCAST ELECTRONICS
4100 North 24th Street
Quincy, IL 62301

BRYSTON MANUFACTURING, LIMITED
57A Westmore Drive
Rexdale, Ontario
Canada M9V 3Y6

BRYSTONVERMONT
RFD 4, Berlin
Montpelier, VT 05602

BSC, BENNETT SOUND CORPORATION
PO Box 565
Reseda, CA 91335

BSR (USA) LIMITED
Route 303
Blauvelt, NY 10913

■

CANNON—TLS
11151 Trade Center Drive
Suite D
Rancho Cordova, CA 95670

CANTON NORTH AMERICA
254 First Avenue North
Minneapolis, MN 55401

CARVER CORPORATION
PO Box 664
14034 NE 193 Place
Woodinville, WA 98072

CELESTION INDUSTRIES
PO Box 521
Kuniholm Drive
Holliston, MA 01746

CERWIN-VEGA, INCORPORATED
12250 Montague Street
Arleta, CA 91331

CLARION CORPORATION OF AMERICA
5500 Rosecrans Boulevard
Lawndale, CA 90260

CLARKE SYSTEMS, INCORPORATED
359C Governors Highway
South Windsor, CT 06074

CM LABS
8000 Madison Pike
Madison, AL 35758

CONCORD ELECTRONICS
8025 Yolanda Avenue
Tarzana, CA 91356

CONRAD-JOHNSON DESIGN, INCORPORATED
1474 Pathfinder Lane
McLean, VA 22101

COVEX COMPANY
675-D Conger Street
Eugene, OR 97402

CRAIG CORPORATION
921 West Artesia Boulevard
Compton, CA 90220

CROWN INTERNATIONAL, INCORPORATED
1718 West Mishawaka Road
Elkhart, IN 46514

■

DAYTON WRIGHT GROUP
97 Newkirk Road North
Richmond Hill, Ontario
Canada L4C 3G4

DB SYSTEMS
Main Street
Rindge Center, NH 03461

dbx
71 Chapel Street
Newton, MA 02195

DBX, INCORPORATED
Route 303
Blauvelt, NY 10913

DCM CORPORATION
670 Airport Boulevard
Ann Arbor, MI 48104

DENNESEN ELECTROSTATICS
PO Box 51
Beverly, MA 01915

DENON
27 Law Drive
Fairfield, NJ 07006

DESIGN ACOUSTICS, INCORPORATED
1221 Commerce Drive
Stow, OH 44224

DESKTOP LOUDSPEAKER SYSTEMS
PO Box 398
Simi Valley, CA 93062

DIRECT SOUND
150 Fifth Avenue
Suite 516
New York, NY 10011

D&K IMPORTS
146 East Post Road
White Plains, NY 10601

DLK ACOUSTICAL PRODUCTS
1405 Mendota Heights Road
St. Paul, MN 55120

DOLPHIN LOUDSPEAKER
PO Box 140
Vashon, WA 98070

DUAL, DIVISION OF ADCOM
11 Elkins Road
East Brunswick, NJ 08816

DUBIE CORPORATION
221 Crane Street
Dayton, OH 45403

DYNAMIC ACOUSTICS
PO Box 646
San Ramon, CA 94583

DYNAMIC ELECTRO ACOUSTICS
3419 Bailey Avenue
Buffalo, NY 14215

DYNAVECTOR SYSTEMS U.S.A.
1721 Newport Circle
Santa Ana, CA 92705

■

EGO SYSTEMS LOUDSPEAKERS
50 Werman Court
Plainview, NY 11803

ELDOLON RESEARCH
PO Box 7717
Ann Arbor, MI 48107

ELECTROCOMPANIET
PO Box 173
Holis, ME 04042

ELECTRON KINETICS
PO Box 596
Lake Havasu City, AZ 86403

ELECTRO-VOICE INCORPORATED, GULTON INDUSTRIES, INCORPORATED
600 Cecil Street
Buchanan, MI 49107

ENTEC
1016 Morse Avenue, #12
Sunnyvale, CA 94086

EPICURE PRODUCTS, INCORPORATED
25 Hale Street
Newburyport, MA 01950

ERCONA CORPORATION
125 Wilbur Place
PO Box 161
Bohemia, NY 11716

ESS, INCORPORATED
9613 Oates Drive
Sacramento, CA 95827

EXPOSURE ELECTRONICS
308-100 West Pender Street
Vancouver, British Columbia
Canada V6B 1R8

■

FINESSE AUDIO PRODUCTS
PO Box 80325
Lincoln, NE 68501

FISHER CORPORATION
21314 Lassen Street
Chatsworth, CA 91311

FOURIER LOUDSPEAKER SYSTEMS
540 Nepperhan Avenue
Yonkers, NY 10701

FRAZIER, INCORPORATED
PO Box 34216
1930 Valley View Lane
Dallas, TX 75234

FRIED PRODUCTS COMPANY
7616 City Line Avenue
Philadelphia, PA 19151

FUJITSU TEN CORPORATION OF AMERICA
19281 Pacific Gateway Drive
Torrance, CA 90502

FULTON MUSICAL INDUSTRIES
4204 Brunswick Avenue North
Minneapolis, MN 55422

FULTRON, ARTHUR FULMER ELECTRONICS DIVISION
PO Box 177
122 Gayoso at 2nd
Memphis, TN 38101

USEFUL ADDRESSES

■

GARRARD U.S.A. INCORPORATED
60 Da Vinci Drive
Bohemia, NY 11716

GC ELECTRONICS
400 South Wyman Street
Rockford, IL 61101

GEM, Sumiko
PO Box 5046
Berkeley, CA 94705

GENERAL ELECTRIC
Electronics Park
Syracuse, NY 13221

GENESIS PHYSICS CORPORATION
Newington Park
Newington, NH 03801

GLI INTEGRATED SOUND SYSTEMS,
SUBSIDIARY VSC CORPORATION
1227 Walt Whitman
Melville, NY 11747

GNP, GROSS NATIONAL PRODUCTS
1244 East Colorado Boulevard
Pasadena, CA 91106

GOETZ SYSTEMS
6800 Roswell Road
Suite 1A
Atlanta, GA 30328

GOLD SOUND
PO Box 141
Englewood, CO 80151

GOLDRING, AUDIOSOURCE
14225 Ventura Boulevard
Sherman Oaks, CA 91423

GOTT LABS
424 Clay Pitts Road
East Northport, NY 11731

GRACE BY SUMIKO
PO Box 5046
Berkeley, CA 94705

GRADO LABORATORIES,
INCORPORATED
4614 Seventh Avenue
Brooklyn, NY 11220

GRAFYX
2201 South Ford
Chicago, IL 60616

GUSDORF CORPORATION
6900 Manchester Avenue
St. Louis, MO 63143

■

HAMMOND INDUSTRIES
8000 Madison Pike
Madison, AL 35758

HARMAN/KARDON, INCORPORATED
240 Crossways Drive West
Woodbury, NY 11797

HARTKE SYSTEMS
42 Orchard Street
Bloomfield, NJ 07003

HARTLEY PRODUCTS CORPORATION
620 Island Road
Ramsey, NJ 07446

HEYBROOK BY MECOM
D'Ascanio Audio
11450 Overseas Highway
Marathon, FL 33050

HITACHI SALES CORPORATION OF
AMERICA
401 West Artesia Boulevard
Compton, CA 90220

■

IAI, INTERNATIONAL AUDIO IMPORTS
723 Bound Brook Road
Dunnellen, NJ 08812

ILLBRUCK/USA
3800 Washington Avenue North
Minneapolis, MN 55412

IMF ELECTRONICS
5226 State Street
Saginaw, MI 48603

IMPORT AUDIO LIMITED
3149 Shenandoah Street
St. Louis, MO 63104

INDUCED MAGNET SYSTEMS (IMS)
115 Henry Street
Freeport, NY 11520

INFINITY SYSTEMS, INCORPORATED
7930 Deering Avenue
Canoga Park, CA 91304

INNOTECH AUDIO SYSTEMS
182 Henry Street
Brooklyn, NY 11201

INNOVATIVE TECHNIQUES
703 Revere Drive
Herbertsville, NJ 08723

INTEGREX, INCORPORATED
PO Box 747
Havertown, PA 19083

INTERAUDIO/BOSE
100 The Mountain Road
Framingham, MA 01701

INTERSEARCH INCORPORATED
4720-Q Boxton Way
Lanham, MD 20801

ITONE AUDIO
1016 Contra Costa Drive
El Cerrito, CA 94530

■

JBL INCORPORATED
8500 Balboa Boulevard
Northridge, CA 91329

JENSEN SOUND LABORATORIES,
DIVISION INTERNATIONAL JENSEN
INCORPORATED, AN ESMARK
COMPANY
4136 North United Parkway
Schiller Park, IL 60176

JRM
3716 Broadway NE
Knoxville, TN 37917

JUMETITE LABORATORIES
1300 Richards Street
Vancouver, British Columbia
Canada V6B 3G6

JVC CORPORATION OF AMERICA
71 Slater Drive
Elmwood Park, NJ 07407

■

KEF ELECTRONICS
425 Sherman Avenue
Suite 130
Palo Alto, CA 94306

KEITH MONKS AUDIO (USA)
INCORPORATED
PO Box 1069
Palatine, IL 60078

KENWOOD ELECTRONICS,
INCORPORATED
1315 E. Watsoncenter Road
Carson, CA 90745

KINDEL AUDIO
1710 Newport Circle
Suite 0
Santa Ana, CA 92705

KINERGETICS INCORPORATED
6029 Reseda Boulevard
Tarzana, CA 91356

KIRKSAETER
4648 Evansdale Road
Woodbridge, VA 22193

KLARK-TEKNIK
262a Eastern Parkway
Farmingdale, NY 11735

KLH RESEARCH & DEVELOPMENT
CORPORATION
7 Powder Horn Drive
Warren, NJ 07060

KLIPSCH & ASSOCIATES
PO Box 688
Hope, AR 71801

KLOSS VIDEO CORPORATION
145 Sidney Street C
Cambridge, MA 02139

KOSS CORPORATION
4129 North Port Washington Avenue
Milwaukee, WI 53212

KRELL INDUSTRIES
1225 Connecticut Avenue
Bridgeport, CT 06607

KRACO ENTERPRISES,
INCORPORATED
505 East Euclid Avenue
Compton, CA 90224

KYOCERA INTERNATIONAL, formerly
Cybernet
7 Powder Horn Drive
Warren, NJ 07060

■

LANCER ELECTRONICS
18350B Ward Street
Fountain Valley, CA 92708

LAKE COMMUNICATIONS,
INCORPORATED
5743 Howard Street
Niles, IL 60648

LAKE, Ercona Corporation
2493 Merrick Road
Bellmore, NY 11710

MARK LEVINSON AUDIO SYSTEMS
2081 South Main Street
Route 17
Middletown, CT 06457

LINEAR POWER, INCORPORATED
11545 Avenue D
Auburn, CA 95603

LINN PRODUCTS LIMITED,
AUDIOPHILE SYSTEMS
6842 Hawthorne Park Drive
Indianapolis, IN 46250

LORANGER MANUFACTURING
CORPORATION
38 Clark Street
Warren, PA 16365

LT SOUND
PO Box 338
Stone Mountain, GA 30086

LUSTRE BY SUMIKO
PO Box 5046
Berkeley, CA 94705

MEDIA DESIGN

LUXMAN, ALPINE ELECTRONICS OF AMERICA
3102 Kashiwa Street
Torrance, CA 90505

■

MAGNAVOX, NORTH AMERICAN PHILIPS
I 40 and Straw Plains Pike
Knoxville, TN 37914

MAGNEPAN, INCORPORATED, MAGNEPLANAR PRODUCTS
1645 9th Street
White Bear Lake, MN 55110

M&K
Miller & Kreisel Sound Corporation
10391 Jefferson Boulevard
Culver City, CA 90230

MARANTZ COMPANY, INCORPORATED
Subsidiary Superscope, Incorporated
20525 Nordhoff Street
Chatsworth, CA 91311

MARK LEVINSON AUDIO SYSTEMS, LIMITED
2081 South Main Street
Route 17
Middletown, CT 06457

JOHN MAROVSKIS AUDIO SYSTEMS
2889 Roebling Avenue
Bronx, NY 10461

MARTIN-LOGAN
320 NE Industrial Lane
Lawrence, KA 66044

MASTERCRAFT AUDIO
PO Box 2661
Huntington Station, NY 11746

MAYWARE
PO Box 58
Edgware, Middlesex
England HA8 9UH

MCINTOSH LABORATORY INCORPORATED
2 Chambers Street
Binghamton, NY 13903

MERIDIAN AUDIO OF AMERICA, MISOBANKE INTERNATIONAL, INCORPORATED
PO Box 653
Buffalo, NY 14240

METRON, DIVISION OF CERWIN-VEGA
12250 Montague Street
Arleta, CA 91331

MICRO-ACOUSTICS CORPORATION
8 Westchester Plaza
Elmsford, NY 10523

MICROFIDELITY
14 Van Zant Street
Norwalk, CT 06855

MICRO SEIKI, SAE
PO Box 60271, Terminal Annex
701 East Macy Street
Los Angeles, CA 90012

MIDLAND INTERNATIONAL CORPORATION
PO Box 1903
Kansas City, MO 64141

MIRAGE ACOUSTICS
850 Rear Providence Highway
Dedham, MA 02026

MISSION ELECTRONICS
310 Carlingview Drive
Rexdale, Ontario
Canada M9W 5G1

MITOM INDUSTRIES
1140 Eighth Line
Oakville, Ontario
Canada L6H 2R4

MITCHELL SPEAKER COMPANY,
Quick Marketing
117-F Riverside Avenue
Newport Beach, CA 92663

MITSUBISHI ELECTRIC SALES AMERICA, Home Audio
3030 East Victoria Street
Rancho Dominguez, CA 90221

MODULAR AUDIO PRODUCTS
50 Orville Dr.
Airport International Plaza
Bohemia, NY 11716

KEITH MONKS AUDIO
PO Box 1069
Palatine, IL 60078

MONSTER CABLE
101 Townsend Street
San Francisco, CA 94107

MOREL ACOUSTICS
414 Harvard Street
Brookline, MA 02146

MTX ELECTRONICS, INCORPORATED
805 Woodman Avenue
Winslow, IL 61089

MXR INNOVATIONS
740 Driving Park Avenue
Rochester, NY 14613

■

NAD (USA), INCORPORATED
675 Canton Street
Norwood, MA 02062

NAGAOKA BY MICROFIDELITY
14 Van Zant Street
Norwalk, CT 06855

NAGATRON, NAGATRONICS CORPORATION
115 Henry Street
Freeport, NY 11520

NAGRA MAGNETIC RECORDERS
19 West 44th Street
New York, NY 10036

NAKAMICHI USA CORPORATION
1101 Colorado Avenue
Santa Monica, CA 90401

NEC HOME ELECTRONICS
1401 West Estes Avenue
Elk Grove Village, IL 60007

NESTOROVIC LABS
8307 NE 110th Place
Kirkland, WA 98033

NEUMANN, GOTHAM AUDIO CORPORATION
741 Washington Street
New York, NY 10014

NEW YORK AUDIO LABORATORIES
33 North Riverside Avenue
Croton-on-Hudson, NY 10520

NIKKO ELECTRIC CORPORATION OF AMERICA
7801 E. Compton Boulevard
Paramount, CA 90723

Oser Avenue
Hauppauge, NY 11787

NILES AUDIO CORPORATION
PO Box 160818
Miami, FL 33116

13824 SW 142nd Avenue
Miami, FL 33116

NORTRONICS COMPANY, INCORPORATED, RECORDER CARE DIVISION
8101 10th Avenue North
Minneapolis, MN 55427

NOVA ELECTRO-ACOUSTICS
PO Box 25488
Los Angeles, CA 90025

NOVAK LOUDSPEAKER
Merritts Island Road
Pine Island, NY 10969

NUMARK ELECTRONICS
503 Raritan Center
Edison, NJ 08817

■

OHM ACOUSTICS CORPORATION
241 Taffe Place
Brooklyn, NY 11205

OMNISONIX, LIMITED
PO Box 430
Middletown Avenue
Northford, CT 06472

ONKYO U.S.A. CORPORATION
200 Williams Drive
Ramsey, NJ 07446

ORBAN ASSOCIATES
645 Bryant Street
San Francisco, CA 94107

ORTOFON
122 Dupont Street
Plainview, NY 11803

O'SULLIVAN INDUSTRIES INCORPORATED
19th and Gulf Streets
Lamar, MO 64759

OTARI CORPORATION
2 Davis Drive
Belmont, CA 94002

■

PAC, PERFECTIONIST AUDIO COMPONENTS
172 Ocean Avenue
Lynnbrook, NY 11563

PANASONIC, DIVISION MATSUSHITA ELECTRIC CORPORATION OF AMERICA
One Panasonic Way
Secaucus, NJ 07094

PARASOUND PRODUCTS
Wharfside
680 Beach Street
Suite 414
San Francisco, CA 94109

PENTAGRAM LOUDSPEAKER COMPANY
207-19 35th Avenue
Bayside, NY 11361

PHASE LINEAR
4134 North United Parkway
Schiller Park, IL 60176

PHILIPS, AKG ACOUSTICS INCORPORATED
77 Selleck Street
Stamford, CT 06902

PHOENIX SYSTEMS
91 Elm Street
Manchester, CT 06040

USEFUL ADDRESSES

PICKERING & COMPANY, INCORPORATED
101 Sunnyside Boulevard
Plainview, NY 11803

PIONEER ELECTRONICS OF AMERICA
5000 Airport Plaza Drive
Long Beach, CA 90815

PIONEER VIDEO
200 West Grand Avenue
Montvale, NJ 07645

PML, ERCONA CORPORATION
125 Wilbur Place
PO Box 161
Bohemia, NY 11716

PRECISION FIDELITY
1131 SE Umatilla Street
Portland, OR 97202

PREMIER BY SUMIKO
PO Box 5046
Berkeley, CA 94705

PRO-ACOUSTICS
Waterfront Plaza
Newport, VT 05855

PROMETHEAN AUDIO PRODUCTS
130 East Winnick
Las Vegas, NV 89109

PROTON CORPORATION
19600 Magellan Drive
Torrance, CA 90502

PSE, PROFESSIONAL SYSTEMS ENGINEERING
2021 West County Rd. C
St. Paul, MN 55113

PYLE INDUSTRIES, INCORPORATED
501 Center Street
Huntington, IN 46750

PYRAMID LOUDSPEAKER
131-15 Fowler Avenue
Flushing, NY 11355

■

QUAD
425 Sherman Avenue
Palo Alto, CA 94036

■

RCA CONSUMER ELECTRONICS
600 North Sherman Drive
Indianapolis, IN 46201

RCS AUDIO INTERNATIONAL
1055 Thomas Jefferson Street
Washington, D.C. 20007

REALISTIC, DIVISION; TANDY CORPORATION
1300 One Tandy Center
Fort Worth, TX 76102

RECOTON CORPORATION
46-23 Crane Street
Long Island City, NY 11101

REFERENCE AUDIO IMPORTS
1215 Audrey Avenue
Campbell, CA 95008

RG DYNAMICS
4448 West Howard Street
Skokie, IL 60076

RGR, ROBERT GRODINSKY RESEARCH
6440 North Ridgeway Avenue
Lincolnwood, IL 60645

REVOX, STUDER REVOX AMERICA, INCORPORATED
1425 Elm Hill Pike
Nashville, TN 37210

RKO TAPE CORPORATION
3 Fairfield Crescent
West Caldwell, NJ 07006

RMI, Reference Monitor International
6074 Corte Del Cedro
Carlsbad, CA 92008

ROBERTSON AUDIO
PO Box 8449
Van Nuys, CA 91409

ROBINS DIVISION, BENJAMIN ELECTROPRODUCTS, INCORPORATED
75 Austin Boulevard
Commack, NY 11725

ROGERSOUND LABS
8381 Canoga Avenue
Canoga Park, CA 91304

RTR INDUSTRIES, INCORPORATED
8116 Deering Avenue
Canoga Park, CA 91034

RTS SYSTEMS
1100 West Chestnut Street
Burbank, CA 91506

■

SAE, SCIENTIFIC AUDIO ELECTRONICS, INCORPORATED
7011 Macy Street
Los Angeles, CA 90012

PO Box 60271 Terminal Annex
Los Angeles, CA 90060

SANSUI ELECTRONICS CORPORATION
1250 Valley Brook Avenue
Lyndhurst, NJ 07071

SANYO ELECTRIC INCORPORATED
1200 West Artesia Boulevard
Compton, CA 90220

SARAS OF AMERICA
13101 Yukon Avenue
Hawthorne, CA 90250

S.C.D., SOMETHING COMPLETELY DIFFERENT
3016 NE Oregon Street
Portland, OR 97232

SCHOEPS, POSTHORN RECORDINGS
142 West 26th Street, 10th Floor
New York, NY 10001

H.H. SCOTT, INCORPORATED
20 Commerce Way
Woburn, MA 01888

SCHUG ELECTRONICS
Box 385
Woodland Hills, CA 91365

SENNHEISER ELECTRONICS CORPORATION
10 West 37th Street
New York, NY 10018

SEQUERRA
3000 Druid Park Drive
Baltimore, MD 21215

SHAHINIAN ACOUSTICS LIMITED
24 Commercial Boulevard
Medford, NY 11763

SHARP ELECTRONICS CORPORATION
10 Keystone Place
Paramus, NJ 07652

SHERWOOD, DIVISION OF INKEL CORPORATION
500 East Carson Plaza Drive
Suite 221
Carson, CA 90745

SIEFERT-MAY LABS
31316 Via Colinas, #103
Westlake Village, CA 91362

SIGNET DIVISION, DIVISION A-T.U.S. INCORPORATED
1221 Commerce Drive
Stow, OH 44224

SINGER PRODUCTS
875 Merrick Avenue
Westbury, NY 11590

SNELL ACOUSTICS
10 Prince Place
Newburyport, MA 01950

SONIC RESEARCH
27 Sugar Hollow Road
Danbury, CT 06810

SONOGRAPHE
1131 SE Umatilla Street
Portland, OR 97202

SONUS BY SONIC RESEARCH, INCORPORATED
27 Sugar Hollow Road
Danbury, CT 06810

SONY INDUSTRIES
Sony Drive
Park Ridge, NJ 07656

SOTA INDUSTRIES
PO Box 7075
Berkeley, CA 94707

SOUND CONCEPTS INCORPORATED
PO Box 135
Brookline, MA 02146

SOUNDCRAFTSMEN
2200 South Ritchey
Santa Ana, CA 92705

SOUND DYNAMICS, AUDIO PRODUCTS INTERNATIONAL
161 Don Park Road
Markham, Ontario
Canada L3R 1C2

SOUND GUARD CORPORATION
348 SW 13th Avenue
Pompano Beach, FL 33060

SOUND RESEARCH
1000 East Del Amo Boulevard
Carson, CA 90746

SOUTHER ENGINEERING
429 York Street
Canton, MA 02021

SPEAKERLAB, INCORPORATED
735 North Northlake Way
Seattle, WA 98103

SPECTRAL AUDIO ASSOCIATES
PO Box 4475
Mountain View, CA 94042

SPECTRASCAN
5923 North Nevada Avenue
Colorado Springs, CO 80907

SPECTRUM LOUDSPEAKERS
Box 2774
Toledo, OH 43606

SPICA
2886-A Trades West Road
Santa Fe, NM 87501

STANTON MAGNETICS, INCORPORATED
Terminal Drive
Plainview, NY 11803

DESIGN

STAX KOGYO
940 East Dominguez
Carson, CA 90746

STRELLOFF SYSTEM DESIGNS
5305 Tendilla Avenue
Woodland Hills, CA 91364

STUDER REVOX AMERICA,
INCORPORATED
1425 Elm Hill Pike
Nashville, TN 37210

SUMIKO
PO Box 5046
Berkeley, CA 94705

SUPEREX ELECTRONICS
151 Ludlow Street
Yonkers, NY 10705

SUPERSCOPE BY MARANTZ
Superscope, Incorporated
20525 Nordhoff Street
Chatsworth, CA 91311

SUPEX BY SUMIKO, INCORPORATED
PO Box 5046
Berkeley, CA 94705

SWITCHCRAFT, INCORPORATED
5555 North Elston Avenue
Chicago, IL 60630

SYMDEX AUDIO SYSTEMS
PO Box 8037
Boston, MA 02114

SYMMETRIC SOUND SYSTEMS
856 Lynn Rose Court
Santa Rosa, CA 95404

■

TAMANTON SOUNDWORKS
440 Broadway
Brooklyn, NY 11211

TANDBERG
Labriola Court
Armonk, NY 10504

TANNEY
c/o Crown Acoustics Limited
97 Victoria Street North
Kitchener, Ontario
Canada N2H 5C1

TASCAM BY TEAC CORPORATION OF
AMERICA
7733 Telegraph Road
Montebello, CA 90640

TDK ELECTRONICS CORPORATION
12 Harbor Park Drive
Port Washington, NY 11050

TEAC CORPORATION OF AMERICA
7733 Telegraph Road
Montebello, CA 90640

TECHNICS, PANASONIC COMPANY,
DIVISION OF MATSUSHITA ELECTRIC
CORPORATION OF AMERICA
One Panasonic Way
Secaucus, NJ 07094

TEKNIKA ELECTRONICS
CORPORATION
1633 Broadway
New York, NY 10019

TELEDYNE BY OLSEN ELECTRONICS
260 South Forge Street
Akron, OH 44327

THIEL AUDIO PRODUCTS COMPANY
4158 Georgetown Road
Lexington, KY 40511

THORENS, EPICURE PRODUCTS
INCORPORATED
25 Hale Street
Newburyport, MA 01950

3D ACOUSTICS
175 Heritage Avenue
Portsmouth, NH 03801

TIBL ELECTRONICS
1721 Newport Circle
Santa Ana, CA 92705

TOSHIBA AMERICA, INCORPORATED
82 Totowa Road
Wayne, NJ 07470

TRANS-AUDIO
505, Boulevard Industriel
Sherbrooke, Quebec
Canada J1L 1X7

■

UHER BY WALTER ODEMER COMPANY,
INCORPORATED
1516 West Magnolia Boulevard
Burbank, CA 91506

ULTRAPHONICS
622 Route 10
Whippany, NJ 07891

UNITRONEX CORPORATION
1711 Landmeier Road
Elk Grove Village, IL 60007

UREI
8500 Balboa Boulevard
Northridge, CA 91329

URSA MAJOR, INCORPORATED
Box 18
Belmont, MA 02178

■

VANDERSTEEN AUDIO
116 West 4th Street
Hanford, CA 93230

VECTOR RESEARCH
20600 Nordhoff Street
Chatsworth, CA 91311

VIBE ACOUSTICS
107 Manchester Drive
Staten Island, NY 10312

VIDAIRE ELECTRONICS
MANUFACTURING CORPORATION
150 Buffalo Avenue
Freeport, NY 11520

VIDICRAFT
0704 SW Bancroft Street
Portland, OR 97201

VISONIK OF AMERICA,
INCORPORATED
701 Heinz Avenue
Berkeley, CA 94710

VPI INDUSTRIES
PO Box 159
Ozone Park, NY 11417

■

WALD SOUND INCORPORATED
11131 Dora Street
PO Box 1085
Sun Valley, CA 91352

WHARFEDALE, RANK HI-FI,
INCORPORATED
291 Strawtown Road
West Nyack, NY 10944

WILSON AUDIO SPECIALTIES
655 Louise Avenue
Novato, CA 94947

■

YAMAHA INTERNATIONAL
CORPORATION
6600 Orangethorpe Avenue
Buena Park, CA 90620

■

ZENITH RADIO CORP.
1000 Milwaukee Ave.
Glenview, IL 60025

Bibliography

Allison, Roy F. "Influence of Listening Rooms on Loudspeaker Systems," *Audio* (August, 1979).

Audio: Your New World of Listening. Washington, D.C.: Electronics Industries Association, Consumer Electronics Group, 1983.

Berstein, Herman. "Understanding Equalization and Time Constants," *Audio* (February, 1982).

Blumenthal, Howard J. *The Media Room: Creating Your Own Entertainment and Information Center.* New York: Penguin, 1983.

Braun, Hugh. *Introduction to English Medieval Architecture,* 2nd ed. New York: Praeger, 1968.

Burton, Ernest James. *The British Theater 1100–1900: Its Repertory and Practice.* London: Jenkins, 1960.

Conant, Kenneth John. *Carolingian and Romanesque Architecture, 800–1200.* Baltimore: Penguin Books, 1959.

Consumer Electronics Annual Review: 1983 Edition Industry Facts and Figures. Washington, D.C.: Electronics Industries Association, Consumer Electronics Group, 1983.

Cook, Olive. *The English House Through Seven Centuries.* London: Nelson, 1968.

Fielding, Alan. "The Listening Room: The Forgotten Component," *High Fidelity* (July, 1979).

Fowler, John, and John Cornforth. *English Decoration in the 18th Century.* Princeton, N.J.: Pyne Press, 1974.

Girouard, Mark. *Life in the English Country House: A Social and Architectural History.* New Haven: Yale University Press, 1978.

———. *Robert Smythson and the Architecture of the Elizabethan Era.* South Brunswick, N.J.: Barnes, 1967.

———. *The Victorian Country House.* New Haven: Yale University Press, 1979.

Godfrey, Walter H. *The Story of Architecture in England, 12th–14th Century.* New York and London: Harper and Brothers, 1931.

Gotch, John Alfred. *The English Home from Charles I to George IV: Its Architecture, Decoration and Garden Design.* London: B.T. Batsford Ltd., 1919.

Graf, Wend, and Michael Levey. *Art and Architecture of the 18th Century in France.* Harmondsworth, England: Penguin Books, Pelican History of Art, 1972.

Henderson, Andrew. *The Family House in England.* London: Phoenix House, 1964.

Minoli, Daniel. "Digital Techniques in Sound Reproduction," Parts I and II, *Audio* (April and May, 1980).

Mitchell, Peter W. "Exotic Loudspeakers I Have Known," *Stereo Review* (August, 1978).

Moore, Charles Herbert. *The Development and Character of Gothic Architecture.* London and New York: Macmillan and Co., 1890.

"Multidimensional Audio," *B&K Instruments Inc. Application Notes.* Bruel and Kjaer Precision Instruments. Paper presented at AES Convention, New York, 1977.

Queen, Dan. "The Importance of Speaker Directivity," *Audio* (September, 1979).

Ray Jr., Ph.D., A. Joseph. "How We Hear," *Audio* (May, 1977).

Sioles, George. "Some Straight Talk on Speaker Design," *Stereo Review* (August, 1977).

Stock, Gary. "Alternative Speaker Technologies," *Audio* (August, 1980).

Thornton, Peter. *17th-Century Interior Decoration in England, France and Holland.* New Haven: Published for the Paul Mellon Centre for Studies in British Art by Yale University Press, 1978.

Turner, Jacob C. "What You Don't Know Hurts," *Audio* (May, 1977).

Video: Your New Window on the World. Washington, D.C.: Electronics Industries Association, Consumer Electronics Group, 1983.

Whyte, Bert. "Behind the Scenes," *Audio* (June, 1978).

Wickham, Glynne William Gladstone. *The Elizabethan Stage, 1300–1660.* Vol. I, *1300–1576.* London: Routledge and Paul; New York: Columbia University Press, 1959.

Index

A
Aarnio, Eero, 54
acoustic aesthetics, 11, 149, 152, 153, 156
acoustic integrity, 156, 158, 161
Acoustic Research, 143
ADA, 77, 132
ADC, 67
ADS, 34, 46, 59
Advent, 101
AIWA, 87, 111
Akai, 33, 67, 95
Allison, 72
AM, 22, 163
AM suppression, 158
amplification and tone controls, 159–160
amplifier, 24, 25, 31, 33, 34, 50, 52, 60, 72, 77, 84, 87, 88, 95, 101, 111, 115, 117, 121, 122, 132, 140, 143, 156, 161, 163; placement of, 156
anechoic chamber, 24
Antine, Tony, 138–139
architecture and social practices, 7–11, 29
audio accessories, 26–27
Audio Command, 33, 52, 70, 71, 95, 101, 112, 121, 151, 155
audio components, 23–27; basic systems, 24–26; selection of, 157–158. See also individual components
Audio Consultant, The, 50, 56, 87, 157
Audio Control, 77
Audio Design Associates, 132
audio for television, 18
audio inputs, 16, 17, 19, 108
audio outputs, 16
audiotext, 163
audio-visual consultant, 32, 33, 34, 43, 46, 50, 52, 56, 64, 70, 72, 87, 88, 95, 101, 112, 132, 136, 139, 143; explanation of, 150

B
background listener, 149, 156, 158
Bacon, Francis, 33
B & W, 25, 34, 50
Bang & Olufsen, 36, 37, 49, 52, 56, 101, 115, 117, 121
bass performance, 153, 154, 160, 161
bedrooms, 44–45, 51, 54, 81, 91, 94–97, 108–109, 110–111, 134–135, 136
Bell and Howell, 78
Bernard, Eric, 94–95, 112–113
Beta, 20, 163. See also VHS; videocassette recorders
Bevridge, Francesca, 95
BIC, 69
Bielecky Brothers, 78
black level, 16–17
Blau, Doris, 121
Bonaventure, 70
"boom," 153
Bose, 115, 117
Botero, Fernando, 80–81
Boulton, 78, 81
Braun, 95
Bray, Robert, 34–35, 72–73
Bray-Schaible Design, Inc., 34–35, 58–59, 153
Bredos, Marcel, 142–143
Breuer, Marcel. See Marcel Breuer chairs
Brno chairs, 60, 144, 145
Bromley, Scott, 110-111
BSR, 117

C
cable television, 18, 19, 23; box for, 31, 56, 68, 69, 98, 99
Cagli, Carrado, 66, 68
Calder, Nicholas, 104–105
camcorder, 20
Canton, 50, 52, 132
Cassatt, Mary, 40
cassette. See tape recorders; videocassettes
Cataffo, Lou, 102–103
CED (Capacitance Electronic Disc), 21
Celestion, 33
Christopher, Karl, 118–119, 161
church, design influence of, 7
Clark, Dave, 34, 72
Club Med, 118–119, 161
Commodore, 46
community antenna television (CATV), 17
compact disc player, 18, 26, 77, 156, 163; mounting of, 155. See also digital disc players
compact discs (CD), 24
compressor/expander units, 163
computers, 11, 16, 17, 22–23, 46, 71, 78, 95, 126, 129, 132, 163
configuration and mounting, 154–156
continuous current carrying capacity, 161
control panels, 33, 34, 52, 56, 64, 69, 71, 77, 78, 83, 87, 92, 95, 101, 111, 136, 157, 163. See also remote controls
convergence, 16, 17
critical listener, 149, 152, 156, 157, 158
critical variables (of a system), 149
crossover, 72

D
damping. See soundproofing
Daylite, 78
"dead" space, 152
Dean, Graham, 49
Deluermoz, Henri, 112
Denon, 95
de Saavedra, Rubén, 76–81
de Santis, Michael, 52–53, 151
design basics, 149–163
Designed Sound, 46, 139, 158
Dexter Design, Inc., 50–51, 56–57, 86–87, 157
digital audio discs (DAD), 23, 24, 26. See also compact discs
digital disc players, 23, 24, 56, 95. See also compact disc players
"digital ready" speakers, 26
Dill, Lesley, 39
dining rooms, 10, 42–43, 113, 114, 137
discrete vs. centralized systems, 156–157
distortion, 158
distortion-free sound, 24
Donghia, Angelo, 32–33, 100–101
Dual, 49, 132
dubbing, 18
Dubuffet, Jean, 39
D'Urso, Joseph, 117
dynamic-range expanders, 26–27
dynamic speakers, 159. See also speakers

E
Edison, Thomas, 24
eigentones, 26
Eileen Gray side table, 63, 125, 129
electronic entertainment. See home entertainment
electronic "hearth," 11
electronic mail, 23
electrostatic speakers, 158–159. See also speakers
English country house, 7
ENIAC (Electronic Numerical Integrator and Calculator), 22
entertainment, 7, 10. See also home entertainment
"entertainment room," 11
equalizers, 26, 31, 52, 67, 77, 95, 115, 156, 160, 163; definition of, 160
equipment placement, 11. See also individual components

F
Falkener, Rita, 88–89, 140–141
family room, 10–11, 36–37
Fawkes, Judith Toxson, 140
feedback, 157
Fidelity Research, 72
'Fledermaus' chairs, 140
flush-mounting, 33, 34, 35, 40, 41, 44, 49, 50, 52, 58, 60, 63, 65, 66, 67, 68, 69, 70, 71, 72, 74, 75, 78, 84, 88, 95, 98, 99, 100, 101, 111, 112, 115, 118, 119, 122, 132, 136, 137, 139, 142; definition of, 154–155, 156
FM, 18, 19, 26, 35
forced vibration, 152
Freeman Theatre Service, 106
Freidman, Barry, 71
frequency response, 17, 158, 163
Friedman, Stanley Jay, 70–71
furnishings, and technology, 11

G
galleries, 7, 8, 9–10
games, 9, 10, 11; video, 16, 23, 146; videodisc, 22
General Electric, 63, 87
Gensler and Associates, 74–75
Gevis, Joel C., 70–71
Gray, Eileen. See Eileen Gray side table
great chambers, 7, 8–9
great halls, 9, 10
Guttilla, Carolyn, 130–131
Gwathmey Siegel Associates, 106–107, 136–137
'Gyro' chairs, 54

H
history, 7–13
Hitachi, 60
Hoffmann, Josef, 106, 112, 122, 140
home entertainment, 7, 8, 11, 13, 16, 17; industry, 11

I
image enhancers, 163
image reproduction, 16
interactive programs (videodisc), 22
International Audio Company, 88

J
Jackson, Dakota, 121
Jacobsen, Robin, 110–111
Jantzen, Arthur, 158
JBL, 72
Jeffrey, Noel, 36–37, 98–99
jukebox, 11
JVC, 36, 50, 95

K
Katz, Alex, 56
Kaypro, 22
Kelly, Ellsworth, 115, 117
Kenwood, 77
KES, 122
kitchens, 65, 67, 69, 104–105, 140–141
Kloss, 92, 125, 134

INDEX

Knoll chairs, 43
Knuckles, Jim, 95
Koitsu, 72
Kripacz, Francisco, 114–117
Kuhn, Gerald, 48–49

L

laserdiscs, 22, 46, 77
Lautrec, Toulouse, 50
Lawrence, Jack Debman, 64–69
Leclerc, Helen, 8
Les Prismatiques, 52
Levinson, Mark, 72
libraries, 7, 8, 9–10, 33, 36, 46–47, 77, 86–87, 139
lighting, 11, 38, 48, 50, 52, 55, 59, 65, 68, 69, 71, 74, 76, 77, 95, 97, 101, 104, 106, 108, 109, 112, 118, 119, 144, 156, 158; guidelines for, 161–162
linearity, 10, 17
listener fatigue, 159
listening room, 24, 26, 150–154, 160. *See also* room shape
"live" space, 152
living rooms, 8, 10, 34, 38, 42–43, 48–49, 50, 52, 56–57, 90, 100–101, 108, 112, 142–143, 144–145, 146–147
Lo Cicero, Mario, 54–55
Lopata, Sam, 38–39
loudspeakers. *See* speakers
Luxman, 25
LV (Laser-Vision), 21
Lyric Hi-Fi, 43

M

Magneplanar, 72
Magritte, René, 136
maintenance, of audio equipment, 27
Mallory, Stephen, 132–133
M & K, 143
manufacturer's specifications, 19, 150, 153
Marantz, 132
Marcel Breuer chairs, 43, 111, 125
McCoy, Michael, 126–129
McIntosh, 49, 50
media basics, 15–27
media rooms, 7, 11, 29–147
Metzger, Robert, 46–47, 120–121, 158
microcomponents, 26, 50, 87, 144, 163
microwave delivered television (MDS TV), 17
Mitsubishi, 20, 46, 50
modems, 23
monitor: placement of, 156; sound, 34, 50, 77; video, 16, 17, 18, 23, 33, 46, 50, 56, 71, 77, 84, 87, 111, 115, 117, 118, 121, 122, 140, 156. *See also* computers; televisions
Montoya, Juan, 42–43, 62–63, 124–125, 134–135, 155, 158
moving coil cartridge, 27
music rooms, 7, 10
Myers, Douglas, 108–109

N

Nakamichi, 25, 56, 72, 78, 84, 121
NEC, 19, 56
Neil, Holly, 64
Nevelson, Louise, 37
"noise," 17
noise-reduction units, 26, 46, 163

O

offices, 54, 70–71, 74–75, 102–103, 118–119, 126–129, 142–143; design history of, 163

Okino, Mimi, 140
Onkyo, 67
ONN Electronics, 88
optimizers (audio), 27
Origines italiennes de l'architecture theatrale moderne, Les, 8
Osbert, Alphonse, 71
oscilloscope, 72
overscan, 16

P

Pace, 38, 52, 77
pantry, 35
Patino, Bob, 60–61, 84–85, 144–145
Perry, Lilla Cabot, 40
personal computers *See* computers
Phase Linear, 132
phasing, 161
Philco, 12
Phillips (North American), 88
phonograph, 11, 12, 24. *See also* turntable
Picasso, Pablo, 66, 68
Pioneer, 16, 21, 46, 77, 131, 143
Polo, Mark, 138–139
Pontez, Hal, 27, 50, 56, 87
Powers, Art, 46, 139, 158
preamplifier, 26, 27, 31, 50, 52, 77, 84, 87, 88, 95, 101, 115, 121, 122, 143, 156, 163
prerecorded videocassettes, 22
processors: audio, 27; video, 27, 77
program sources, 11, 18, 24, 26
project designs, 29–147
projection screen, 54, 55, 77–78, 79, 95, 102, 134. *See also* projection television
projection television, 18–19, front, 18, 19; guidelines, 160; large-screen, 18, 29, 77, 83, 92, 125, 134, 139; rear, 18, 19, 63; single-tube, 18; three-tube, 18
projector, 54, 55, 62, 78, 101, 102, 125, 134, 139
Proton, 17
psychoacoustical disorientation, 152
Pyramid, 50

R

rack-mounting, 154; definition of, 155
radio, 11, 12, 24, 78, 108, 111
Ransgate, 13
RCA, 12, 13, 18, 49, 77, 87, 98, 146
receiver, 25, 26, 49, 50, 56, 67, 69, 78, 87, 131
record player. *See* phonograph; turntable
remote controls, 18, 34, 40, 41, 68, 87, 88, 95, 117, 136, 157. *See also* control panels
resonances, 150, 154
retreats, 40–41, 84–85, 122
reverberation, 24, 26, 27, 152, 160
RGB input, 23
room shape, 150, 151, 156, 160
Ross, Barbara, ASID, 50–51, 56–57, 86–87
Rotel, 125

S

SAE, 34, 52, 115, 121, 143
Sansui, 33, 52, 69, 143
satellite reception, 16, 18, 23
Schaible, Michael, 34, 35, 72–73
Schwartz, Barbara, ASID, 50–51, 56–57, 86–87
screening rooms, 11, 29, 54–55, 78, 106–107, 118–119, 161
Scruggs, Allen, 108–109
seating arrangement, 11, 156, 157
Seff, Ron, 121

shelf-mounting, 42, 50, 56, 58, 59, 69, 77, 122, 131, 144, 145, 154; defined, 155–156
Shumaker, Cliff, 27, 50, 56, 87
signal sources (audio), 26
signal-to-noise ratio, 158, 163
simulcast television, 18
simultaneous audio, 34, 46, 56, 64, 132, 158
simultaneous video, 40, 146
Snyder, David, 146–147
software, 22, 23
Sony, 23, 25, 31, 36, 40, 41, 46, 50, 54, 56, 60, 68, 69, 77, 81, 83, 84, 87, 98, 101, 108, 111, 115, 117, 121, 122, 132, 140, 146
sound-absorbing decor, 152
Sound Concepts, 72
Soundcraftsmen, 88
soundproofing, 106, 152, 156
sound reproduction, 150
sound walls, 11
speakers, 150, 152, 160, 161; audio, 25, 26, 34, 46, 49, 50, 52, 56, 58, 65, 67, 68, 72, 75, 77, 79, 87, 88, 90, 91, 95, 98, 99, 111, 115, 117, 119, 121, 122, 132, 136, 137, 139, 140, 143; cause of listener fatigue, 159; design, 158–159; efficiency, 160; mounting of, 154, 156; placement of, 153–154; video, 16, 18, 84, 102. *See also* dynamic speakers; electrostatic speakers
Springer, Karl, 121
standing-wave resonance. *See* eigentones
Stella, Frank, 49
Stephens, Katherine, 40–41
Ster-a-mote, 33
stereo imagery, 153
stereos, 24. *See also individual components*; audio components
storage (for records, tapes, etc.), 31, 33, 38, 49, 50, 54, 56, 58, 60, 62, 63, 67, 68, 69, 72, 74, 76, 84, 87, 97, 98, 101, 106, 111, 115, 117, 121, 125, 126, 131, 132, 139
Stratos Hi-Fi, 136
Stuetley, Stan, 88–89, 140–141
Surround Sound, 77
switching systems, 34, 46, 64, 77, 132. *See also* control panels; remote controls

T

tape recorders, 11, 24, 26, 34, 156; cassette, 24, 25, 26, 33, 46, 49, 50, 52, 56, 60, 67, 68, 69, 72, 78, 84, 87, 95, 101, 108, 111, 115, 121, 122, 131, 132, 140, 143, 163; placement of, 156; reel-to-reel, 33, 46, 52, 65, 67, 78, 88, 95, 101, 115, 132, 163; selection of, 157–158
Taylor, Michael, 92–93
TEAC, 34, 46, 52, 67, 88, 95, 101
Technics, 33, 72, 88, 95
telecommunicating, 22
telephones, 34, 40, 68, 69, 71, 77, 84, 95, 117, 163
telephone answering machine, 34
television program sources. *See* program sources
televisions, 11, 12, 16–18, 31, 33, 36, 40, 41, 45, 49, 60, 68, 69, 74, 81, 90, 91, 98, 99, 104, 108, 111, 117, 146. *See also* monitors; projection television
television screens, 16, 63, 100, 101. *See also* projection television
Teletext, 23
Thalia Hi-Fi, 106

Tihany, Adam, 30–31
time-delay systems (audio), 26, 27
Tizio lamps, 111
Tsao Calvin, 122–123
tuners: audio, 24, 25, 26, 31, 33, 34, 35, 46, 50, 52, 60, 68, 87, 88, 95, 101, 111, 115, 117, 121, 132, 140, 156, 163; selection of, 158; video, 16, 17–18, 23, 50, 56, 69, 84, 111, 140, 156
turntables, 24, 25, 26, 33, 34, 38, 46, 50, 52, 56, 65, 69, 72, 78, 84, 95, 101, 115, 117, 121, 122, 131, 132, 156, 163; mounting of, 155, 156; placement of, 156; selection of, 157, 158
TVRO (TV Receive-Only) stations, 23
tweeters, 18, 26, 58, 72, 153

U

University of Pennsylvania, 22
upgrading, of audio components, 26, 154, 155, 156
Urmson, Roger, 70–71

V

van den Nieuwelaar, Aldo, 129
ventilation, 31, 72, 154, 155
VHD (Video High Density), 21
VHS (Video Home System), 20, 50, 163. *See also* Beta; videocassette recorders
vibration, 156
Victorian era, 10
videocassette recorders (VCR), 16, 17, 18, 19–21, 22, 36, 49, 50, 56, 60, 77, 84, 87, 95, 98, 99, 101, 115, 117, 131, 140, 146, 156; features, 20; mounting of, 155; vs. videocassettes, 19–22. *See also* Beta; VHS
videocassettes, 20–21, 22
video components, 16–23; selection of, 157
videodisc players, 16, 19, 21–22, 23, 77; mounting of, 155; vs. videocassette recorders, 19–22
videodiscs, 11, 18, 21–22, 23. *See also* compact discs
video inputs, 16, 17, 19, 108
video outputs, 16, 17
videotape, 19, 23, 74
videotext systems, 16, 23, 163. *See also* Teletext; Viewdata
video vs. television, 17, 18
Vidicraft, 27
Viewdata, 23
'Villa Gallia' chairs, 106–107, 122
visual aesthetics, 11, 158

W

Walker, Kenneth Brian, 90–91
Walker, Peter, 158
wall-mounting, 153
Walz, Kevin, 82–83
Wellworth, Ron, 88
wiring, 11, 65, 67, 154, 160–161
Wolf, Vincent, 60–61, 84–85, 144–145
woofers, 18, 26, 58, 72, 153, 156. *See also* bass performance

Y

Yamaha, 84, 101, 122

Z

Zenith, 31, 33, 49, 77, 98, 111

ABOUT THE AUTHOR
Philip Mazzurco is a New York City based editor and freelance writer, with numerous credits in the design field. As well as being an editor with *Home Entertainment* magazine, he is a contributing editor to *Restaurant Design, Lighting Dimensions,* and *Ultra.* The author has studied at Parsons and the Fashion Institute of Technology in the United States, and abroad at the University of Rome and the University of London. He is a press member of the American Society of Interior Designers.